Specialization and Trade

Specialization and Trade

A RE-INTRODUCTION TO ECONOMICS

Arnold Kling

CATO INSTITUTE
WASHINGTON, D.C.

Library of Congress Cataloging-in-Publication Data

Names: Kling, Arnold S., author.
Title: Specialization and trade : a reintroduction to economics : an introduction / Arnold Kling.
Description: Washington, D.C. : Cato Institute, [2016] | Includes bibliographical references and index.
Identifiers: LCCN 2016017478 (print) | LCCN 2016023070 (ebook) | ISBN 9781944424152 (pbk. : alk. paper) | ISBN 9781944424176 (audiobook : alk. paper) | ISBN 9781944424169 (ebook)
Subjects: LCSH: Economics. | Economic specialization. | International trade.
Classification: LCC HB171 .K545 2016 (print) | LCC HB171 (ebook) | DDC 330—dc23

Printed in the United States of America.

CATO INSTITUTE
1000 Massachusetts Ave., N.W.
Washington, D.C. 20001
www.cato.org

CONTENTS

Foreword

Early in 2015, I came across a volume of essays edited by E. Roy Weintraub titled *MIT and the Transformation of American Economics*.[1] After digesting the essays, I thought to myself, "So *that's* how it all went wrong."

Let me hasten to mention that my own doctorate in economics, which I obtained in 1980, comes from MIT. Also, the writers of Weintraub's book are generally laudatory toward MIT and its influence.

Yet I have come to believe in the wake of the MIT transformation, which began soon after World War II, that economists have lost the art of critical thinking. The critical thinker

---

[1] E. Roy Weintraub, ed., *MIT and the Transformation of American Economics* (Durham, NC: Duke University Press, 2014).

always asks, "How do you know that?" The MIT approach suppresses that question and instead presumes that economic researchers and policymakers are capable of obtaining knowledge that in reality is beyond their grasp.[2] That is particularly the case in the field known as macroeconomics, whose practitioners claim to know how to manage the overall levels of output and employment in the economy.

I have set out to write an introduction to economics as I believe it ought to be studied. It is written primarily for other scholars of economics, to challenge the way that economists now approach their discipline. However, I also want this book to be accessible to students with little or no training in economics, so that early in the process of study, they can be warned about problems with the standard approach and can have some exposure to an alternative.

---

[2] F. A. Hayek made this point forcefully in his Nobel lecture, "The Pretense of Knowledge," December 11, 1974, http://www.nobelprize.org/nobel_prizes /economic-sciences/laureates/1974/hayek-lecture.html.

Acknowledgments

I am an unaffiliated scholar, but I have been influenced at a distance by several members of the faculty at George Mason University. As the financial crisis of 2008 morphed into the Great Recession, Tyler Cowen wrote a blog post using the phrase "'dual' of the socialist calculation problem."[3] In other words, just as a government board cannot obtain or process all of the information necessary to plan an economy, sometimes the market's decentralized adjustment process can be overwhelmed by rapid, broad-based shifts, particularly those that involve financial intermediation. I took this germ of an

---

[3] Tyler Cowen, "The Economic Crisis, the Calculation Debate, and Stability Theory," December 18, 2008, http://marginalrevolution.com/marginalrevolution/2008/12/a-simple-model.html.

idea and grew it into a replacement for mainstream macroeconomics, which I call "patterns of sustainable specialization and trade." That alternative will be included in this volume. On Twitter, Garett Jones posted something to the effect that today's workers are building organizational capital rather than widgets, and that tweet influenced the way that I characterize specialization and roundabout production. Donald Boudreaux has been relentless in emphasizing the remarkable difference between what we can consume relative to what we produce, thanks to specialization and trade. Finally, Pete Boettke likes to draw a distinction between "mainstream economics" and "mainline economics," with what I call MIT economics representing the former and the economics you will find in these pages representing my attempt at the latter.

Many colleagues have provided comments on earlier drafts. Garett Jones put considerable effort into his suggestions, many of which I have taken. Aaron Ross Powell and David Lampo of the Cato Institute helped to shepherd this project along. I also wish to thank Tyler Cowen, Yuval Levin, Alberto Mingardi, and Alex Tabarrok. Neither they nor the Cato Institute is responsible for any errors or misguided opinions that remain.

Introduction

> Observe the accommodation of the most common artificer or day-labourer in a civilized and thriving country, and you will perceive that the number of people of whose industry a part, though but a small part, has been employed in procuring him this accommodation, exceeds all computation.
>
> —Adam Smith, *The Wealth of Nations*

In a primitive society, people are self-sufficient. Each family gathers its own food, makes its own clothing, and finds its own shelter. The largest unit of social cooperation would be an extended family or tribe.

In a modern economy, no one is self-sufficient. Instead, people are specialized. The work you do probably does not produce something you could consume. Even more striking is the fact that almost everything you consume is something you could not possibly produce. Your daily life depends on the cooperation of hundreds of millions of other people.

Just as it is inconceivable that human society would have evolved to its present state without language, it is inconceivable that we would have gotten to this point without specialization and trade. Moreover, in order for society to progress further, patterns of specialization and trade must continue to evolve.

However, specialization and trade are often misunderstood. Misconceptions about specialization and trade are held by economists as well as by noneconomists, by libertarians as well as by socialists. The purpose of this book is to expose and try to correct important misconceptions, especially the misconceptions about specialization and trade, that afflict leading economists and their textbooks.

Picture yourself watching news on cable television while eating a bowl of cereal. However, instead of giving you the news, the TV announcer asks you to consider what you would need to do to make your cereal completely from scratch.

You would need to grow the cereal grains yourself. If you use tools to harvest the grain, you would have to make those tools yourself. To make those tools would require that you yourself mine the metals, process them, combine them, and shape them. To mine the metals, you would have to be able to locate them. You would need machinery, which you would have to build yourself.

Instead of headlines, the "crawl" on the TV lists all of the tasks and people needed to produce your breakfast. Your cereal was manufactured in a factory that had a variety of workers and many machines. People had to manage the factory. Organization of the firm required many functions in finance and administration. First, however, people had to build the factory. The machines used in the factory in turn had to be manufactured. The machines were made out of materials that had to be mined and transported. That transportation required many other people and machines. The transportation equipment itself had to be manufactured, which required mining and shipping materials to the place where the transportation equipment was manufactured.

Look at the list of ingredients in the cereal. Those ingredients had to be refined and shipped to the cereal manufacturer. Again, those processes required many machines, which in turn had to be manufactured. The cereal grains and other ingredients had to be grown, harvested, and processed. Machines were involved in those processes, and those machines had to be manufactured.

Next, the "crawl" goes through a similar exercise for the milk you put on your cereal, for the bowl and the spoon, and for the refrigerator from which you took the milk.

Such a thought experiment can help you grasp the extent of specialization in modern society. We carry on our lives not really conscious of the complexity of that specialization. In fact, when it enters our minds, we often resent it. We praise ourselves for our urban gardens and our do-it-yourself home projects. We urge one another to "buy local," and we berate business executives for moving jobs overseas. Of course, if we took such sentiments to their logical conclusion and tried to eliminate commerce with strangers entirely, we would have to return to primitive hunting and gathering.

Even economists generally lose sight of specialization. We do teach an important concept, called comparative advantage, which shows that with two products and two producers, more total output can be produced when each producer specializes in tasks with which he or she is relatively efficient. Even if the surgeon can mow lawns faster than an unskilled worker, it still makes more sense for her to focus on performing surgery while the unskilled worker mows her lawn.

I want to emphasize that comparative advantage is not the only source of specialization. Consider Cheryl, a fictional computer programmer at a bank, who works on a system to track payments made to the bank by mortgage borrowers. True, her specialized work is based in part on comparative advantage: it is more efficient for the bank to use Cheryl as a programmer and Thomas as a teller than the other way around. However, Cheryl is also a specialist in other senses. Her experience with the bank's particular system means that she specializes in firm-specific knowledge. Her familiarity with mortgage terminology is more useful to a bank than it would be to a company that develops video games. We might say that she specializes by industry. Cheryl also produces no marketable output; instead, the system she works on contributes to the bank's organizational capabilities. We might say that she specializes in an early stage of the production process.

If Cheryl's bank no longer needed a mortgage payment processing system, her value would be reduced. If her bank went completely out of business, her value would be reduced more. If the mortgage servicing industry consolidated, using fewer systems, her value would be reduced more still. And if computers suddenly became much more expensive and banks went back to using mechanical calculators, her value would be reduced still more. That last hypothetical is extreme, but the point is that specialization is subtle, deep, and highly dependent on context. The textbook examples that show specialization arising from comparative advantage are deceptively simple and single faceted.

Unfortunately, once they have taught the simple example of comparative advantage, with two producers and two tasks, most economists are done with the issue of specialization. Instead, textbooks want to focus on scarcity and choice. Often, the student will read that economics is about the allocation of scarce resources given our unlimited wants. Or he or she may be told that economics is the study of how people make rational choices among competing priorities.

Scarcity and choice are certainly important concepts, but making them the central focus can lead to economic analysis that is simplistic and mechanistic. In fact, the approach to economics that took hold after World War II treats the economy as a machine governed by equations. Textbooks using that approach purport to offer a repair manual, with policy tools to fix the economic machine when something goes wrong.

The mechanistic metaphor is inappropriate and even dangerous. A better metaphor would be that of a rainforest. The economy is a complex, evolving system.

Another metaphor would be the Internet, which is also a complex, evolving system. Although the Internet requires hardware, its value lies in its software. The same is true for economies. Economists used to focus on the "hardware" of the economy, such as factories and equipment. More recently, we have come to realize that intangible factors, such as social norms and cumulative innovation, are the important determinants of economic outcomes.

We can also see—if we choose to—the vast web of complex specialization that makes up a modern economy. That vast web gives us many insights and issues to consider:

- Increased wealth accompanies specialization. Our ancestors were much less specialized than we are. As recently as the 18th century, many households still sewed their own clothes, built their own homes, and grew much of their own food. As of 1700, nearly everyone in the world lived in economic misery by today's standards. Even in the United Kingdom, the most advanced economy at the time, the average income per person was only about $2,500 in today's dollars.[4] Today, in the United States, a household would need twice that average income to even reach the

[4] Based on Angus Maddison, *Contours of the World Economy, 1–2030 AD: Essays in Macro-Economic History* (New York: Oxford University Press, 2007). He provides figures in 1990 dollars (https://en.wikipedia.org/wiki/List_of_regions _by_past_GDP_(PPP)_per_capita#World_1.E2.80.932003_.28Maddison.29), which I attempted to convert to 2015 dollars using the change in the U.S. consumer price index.

poverty line. We owe our much greater well-being today to the millions of people who indirectly work to supply us with goods and services in a specialized economy.

- Trade accompanies specialization. The more you specialize, the more you need to trade to obtain what you want. In a society where people specialize, you will find them exchanging goods and services. Those exchanges are what we count as economic activity. The standard measure of economic activity, known as gross domestic product, or GDP, is an attempt to measure the total market value of goods and services that are bought and sold.

- Urbanization accompanies specialization. People in cities need to trade for food, meaning that the urban dwellers must provide goods and services useful for farmers. Urbanization promotes complexity. The more densely people are packed, the greater the degree of specialization that can be accomplished. The historical trend is toward more specialization, more trade, and more urbanization.

- Social complexity increases with specialization. Today's society is tremendously more complex than the society of the 18th century, which in turn was far more complex than hunter-gatherer bands.

- Improvements in transportation accompany specialization. The farther that you can cheaply transport goods, the more specialization you will see. Before the advent of the railroad, water transport was relatively efficient, so that specialization tended to be most extensive near good harbors and navigable rivers. Improvements in transportation have connected the world's regions more closely, promoting greater specialization.

- As Adam Smith pointed out, specialization expands with the extent of the market. As the number of consumers of a good increases, the tasks involved in producing the good can be subdivided further.

- As Smith also pointed out, producers would like to conspire with one another to stifle competition. Because we specialize in production, our well-being is much more affected by changes in the market for what we produce than it is by changes in the market for any one of the many goods and services that we consume. That makes us strongly disposed to favor restrictions that restrict competition in the market where we produce. Although we have a preference for free trade in the markets where we consume, that preference is less focused and less intense. As a consequence, political lobbyists representing producer interests are more heavily engaged than are lobbyists for consumer interests. In turn, that difference can lead to a regulatory process that favors incumbent producers to the detriment of consumers and new would-be producers. That favoritism can be seen in the resistance of many local governments to Uber as an alternative to taxis, Airbnb as an alternative to hotels, or charter schools as an alternative to government-run schools.

- Modern specialization is so extensive that only a minority of people in a modern economy directly provide goods and services for immediate consumption, such as food or medical care. Instead, many of us work in industries that supply intermediate inputs, meaning materials, machines, information, or logistical support for businesses that offer goods and services for direct consumption. And even among those who work in businesses that provide immediate consumer satisfaction, many of us perform administrative tasks to manage or support those workers who actually serve customers.

- Specialization means that we rely on tasks performed by strangers. If we cannot trust what strangers do, then we cannot specialize. For transactions to be trustworthy, markets must be bolstered by social norms and enforcement mechanisms, including a reliable legal system.

- An increase in capital intensity accompanies an increase in specialization. Think of capital as tools that are used to produce things. Farm equipment helps produce food. Manufacturing plants help build farm equipment. Steel and concrete production facilities help build manufacturing plants. Workers with powerful tools are more productive. It is easier to excavate a foundation with a bulldozer than with a spoon.

- Another way of describing capital intensity is that specialization increases the number of steps in the production process. Consider a farmer about to harvest wheat. Before harvesting the wheat, the farmer might need a threshing machine. Before that, a company must assemble the thresher. Before that, a company must make steel for the thresher manufacturer. The steel must be transported, which may require a railroad or a ship for transportation. And so on. Most of the people whose work enables the farmer to harvest wheat have no idea that they are part of the wheat production process. The Austrian school of economics would describe this multistep production process as very roundabout.

- The roundabout process (or high capital intensity) creates a gap of time between the initial steps in the production process and the final sale of goods and services. During that time gap, workers involved in the early stages of the production process must receive income before consumers have made purchases. (Think of the producer of farm equipment, which must receive payment from a farmer before the farmer can use the equipment to harvest a crop.) That precondition requires financial intermediation. As the economy becomes more specialized and the production becomes more roundabout, the financial sector takes on more significance.

- If trade entails trust among strangers, then financial intermediation entails trust over time. If people lose trust in financial intermediaries, then financial intermediation can decline precipitously. That sharp decline can have a broad effect on the structure of production in the economy.

The purpose of this re-introduction to economics is to make specialization the main character in the story. In a sense, it returns economics to its roots in Adam Smith. In *The Wealth of Nations*, Smith famously wrote about a pin factory:

> I have seen a small manufactory of this kind where ten men only were employed, and where some of

them consequently performed two or three distinct operations. But though they were very poor, and therefore but indifferently accommodated with the necessary machinery, they could, when they exerted themselves, make among them about twelve pounds of pins in a day. There are in a pound upwards of four thousand pins of a middling size. Those ten persons, therefore, could make among them upwards of forty-eight thousand pins in a day. Each person, therefore, making a tenth part of forty-eight thousand pins, might be considered as making four thousand eight hundred pins in a day. But if they had all wrought separately and independently, and without any of them having been educated to this peculiar business, they certainly could not each of them have made twenty, perhaps not one pin in a day; that is, certainly, not the two hundred and fortieth, perhaps not the four thousand eight hundredth part of what they are at present capable of performing, in consequence of a proper division and combination of their different operations.[5]

---

[5] Adam Smith, *The Wealth of Nations*, book 1, chapter 1, section 3.

In a related passage, quoted at the beginning of this introduction, Smith continued:

> The woollen coat, for example, which covers the day-labourer, as coarse and rough as it may appear, is the produce of the joint labour of a great multitude of workmen. The shepherd, the sorter of the wool, the wool-comber or carder, the dyer, the scribbler, the spinner, the weaver, the fuller, the dresser, with many others, must all join their different arts in order to complete even this homely production. How many merchants and carriers, besides, must have been employed in transporting the materials from some of those workmen to others who often live in a very distant part of the country! How much commerce and navigation in particular, how many ship-builders, sailors, sail-makers, rope-makers, must have been employed in order to bring together the different drugs made use of by the dyer, which often come from the remotest corners of the world! What a variety of labour too is necessary in order to produce the tools of the meanest of those workmen![6]

[6] Ibid., section 11.

Centuries later, Walter Lippmann wrote:

> The thinker, as he sits in his study drawing his plans
> for the direction of society, will do no thinking if his
> breakfast has not been produced for him by a social
> process which is beyond his detailed comprehension.
> He knows that his breakfast depends upon workers
> on the coffee plantations of Brazil, the citrus groves of
> Florida, the sugar fields of Cuba, the wheat farms of
> the Dakotas, the dairies of New York; that it has been
> assembled by ships, railroads, and trucks, has been
> cooked with coal from Pennsylvania in utensils made
> of aluminum, china, steel, and glass. But the intricacy
> of one breakfast, if every process that brought it to the
> table had deliberately to be planned, would be beyond
> the understanding of any mind. Only because he can
> count upon an infinitely complex system of working
> routines can a man eat his breakfast and then think
> about a new social order.[7]

In my view, that specialization is the most essential fact in economics. Each of us performs only a narrow range of tasks, often

[7] Walter Lippmann, *The Good Society* (New Brunswick, NJ: Transaction Publishers, 1937, 2005), p. 30.

producing nothing that is directly consumable at all, and yet we enjoy goods and services that require hundreds of millions of tasks performed by millions of workers all over the world.

In the sections that follow, I want to expand on the significance of specialization. The phenomenon of specialization helps explain why we observe markets, firms, property rights, money, and finance.

I want to draw particular attention to the way that specialization makes an economy subject to fluctuations in employment and economic activity. Entrepreneurs constantly test new types of specialization, leading to what Joseph Schumpeter called creative destruction, meaning new enterprises that drive old firms out of business. Modern production processes involve many layers and many steps, making the patterns of specialization highly complex. New patterns create new opportunities, but other patterns can become unsustainable.

When patterns of specialization become unsustainable, the individuals affected can face periods of unemployment. They are like soldiers waiting for new orders, except that the orders come not from a commanding general but from the decentralized actions of many entrepreneurs testing ideas in search of profit.

Fluctuations in economic activity may be amplified by feedback involving financial intermediation. Some patterns of specialization and trade depend on the public's trust in financial intermediaries. At times, intermediaries may enjoy more trust than they deserve, enabling them to finance an unsustainable boom. Once the fragility of the intermediaries is exposed, the level of trust falls, and there can be significant adverse consequences for economic activity.

The rest of this book proceeds as follows:

"Filling in Frameworks" wrestles with the misconception that economics is a science. This section looks at the difficulties that economists face in trying to adopt scientific methods. I suggest that economics differs from the natural sciences in that we have to rely much less on verifiable hypotheses and much more on hard-to-verify interpretative frameworks. Economic analysis is a challenge, because judging interpretive frameworks is actually harder than verifying scientific hypotheses.

"Machine as Metaphor" attacks the misconception held by many economists and embodied in many textbooks that the economy can be analyzed like a machine. This section looks at a widely used but misguided approach to economic analysis, treating it as if it were engineering. The economic engineers are stuck in a mindset that grew out of the Second World War, a conflict that was dominated by airplanes, tanks, and other machines. Their approach fails to take account of the many nonmechanistic aspects of the economy.

"Instructions and Incentives" deals with the misconception that economic activity is directed by planners. This section explains that although people within a firm are guided to tasks through instruction from managers, the economy as a whole is not coordinated that way. Instead, the price system functions as the coordination mechanism.

"Choices and Commands" is concerned with the misconceptions held by socialists and others who disparage the market system. This section explains why a decentralized price system can work better than a centralized command system. Central planning faces an information problem, an incentive problem, and an innovation problem.

"Specialization and Sustainability" exposes the misconception that we must undertake extraordinary efforts in order to conserve specific resources. This section explains how the price system guides the economy toward sustainable use of resources. In contrast, individuals who attempt to override the price system through their individual choices or by imposing government regulations can easily miscalculate the costs of their actions.

"Trade and Trust" addresses the misconception among some libertarians that the institutional infrastructure needed to support specialization and trade is minimal. Instead, this section suggests that for specialization to thrive, societies must reward and punish people according to whether they play by rules that facilitate specialization and trade. A variety of cultural norms, civic organizations, and government institutions serve this purpose, but each of those institutions has its drawbacks.

"Finance and Fluctuations" deals with the misconceptions about finance that are common among economists, who often fail to appreciate the process of financial intermediation. This section looks at the special role played by financial intermediaries in enabling specialization. Intermediation is particularly dependent on trust, and as that trust ebbs and flows, the financial sector can amplify fluctuations in the economy's ability to create patterns of sustainable specialization and trade.

"Policy in Practice" corrects the misconception that diagnosis and treatment of "market failure" is straightforward. This section looks at challenges facing economists and policymakers trying to use the theory of market failure. The example I use is housing finance policy during the run-up to the financial crisis of 2008. The policy process was overwhelmed by the complexity of the specialization that emerged in housing finance. Moreover, the basic thrust of policy was determined by interest-group influence. The lesson is that a very large gap exists between the economic theory of public goods and the practical execution of policy.

"Macroeconomics and Misgivings" argues that it is a misconception, albeit one that is well entrenched in the minds of both professional economists and the general public, to think of the economy as an engine with spending as its gas pedal. This section presents an alternative to the mainstream Keynesian and monetarist traditions. I argue that fluctuations in employment arise from changes in the patterns of specialization and trade. Discovering new patterns of sustainable specialization and trade is more complex and subtle and less mechanical than what is assumed by the Keynesian and monetarist traditions.

Filling in Frameworks

Believe those who seek the truth; doubt those who find it.

—André Gide[8]

In 2000, Ursinus College, a small undergraduate institution in Pennsylvania, raised its tuition by more than 17 percent. Subsequently, the number of applicants and acceptances for its freshman class rose.[9] That outcome appears to violate the law of demand,

[8] A number of Internet sites attribute this quotation to Gide, but I have not been able to locate an exact citation.

[9] See Jonathan D. Glater and Allen Finder, "In Tuition Game, Popularity Rises with Price," *New York Times*, December 12, 2006, http://www.nytimes.com/2006/12/12 /education/12tuition.html?n=Top%2FReference%2FTimes%20Topics%2FSubjects.

which says that demand goes down as the price goes up.[10] Has the law of demand been found to be false?

Neither I nor any other economist would be willing to concede that the law of demand fails to hold. Instead, we would look for factors that might account for the Ursinus College application anomaly. For example, we might ask whether competing colleges raised their prices as much as or more than Ursinus. Perhaps Ursinus College had a successful basketball season, or another factor raised its profile among high school students. Perhaps a new government program increased the subsidies for college students.

In fact, the article on Ursinus College mentions that it also raised its level of student aid by close to 20 percent, and that the majority of students paid less than half of the full price. One can argue that, rather than defying the law of demand, Ursinus was using it. The college was taking advantage of what economists call price discrimination, charging a high price to those students willing to pay while luring the more price-sensitive students with generous aid.

---

[10] There is an exception to the law of demand, known as Giffen's Paradox. Supposedly, when the price of potatoes went up in Ireland, Irish people were so impoverished by that rise that they consumed less meat and more potatoes. In what follows, let us agree to ignore this exception. It certainly would not explain the Ursinus College anomaly.

The point is that the law of demand holds only when "all other things are equal." However, in the real world, other things are almost never equal. In the case of Ursinus College, financial aid policies were not being held equal.

In physics or engineering, when you leave out a factor (such as friction), you do so because you can show that in the context of your analysis that factor will not be important. In economics, we typically cannot do that, because we do not control the environment in which we undertake a study. Many important causal factors will be operating at once, and although we might hope or pretend that none of them matter, we often have no basis for ruling out their importance.

When economists seek to explain phenomena, we usually confront a long list of possibly influential factors. Unlike physicists or engineers, we cannot demonstrate that factors are unimportant in order to justify ignoring them. Instead, we are subject to what is known as confirmation bias. That is, we tend to selectively cite observations that confirm our views, ignoring other factors that might be at work. However, when observations appear to confound our views, we seek out and cite those other factors. If its applications had fallen when Ursinus College raised tuition, we would not have looked for other explanations. However, when demand increased, we are inclined to examine other factors.

Is economics a science? Some people, mostly economists, believe that it is. On the other hand, other people, mostly noneconomists, are skeptical or even scornful of what economists teach.

I think that both camps are guilty of underestimating the challenge of arriving at economic understanding. Those economists who claim the mantle of science are guilty of hubris. Noneconomists who think that their own intuition is superior to economic reasoning are dangerously misguided.

Imagine that you had a scale to measure the carefulness with which someone reasons about a subject. Let that scale run from 1 to 5, with 1 representing the most careless sort of reasoning, filled with superstition and personal biases, and 5 representing scientific reasoning, based on mathematical logic and experimental observation. Where does economics fit in?

I believe that good economics is at least a 6! That is, good reasoning in economics requires *more* careful thinking than good physical science—for two reasons. First, more causal factors are at work in economics than in physical science. Second, although physical relationships are relatively stable, the economy evolves rapidly, including evolution in response to government's attempts at regulation.

A key component of the scientific method is making statements that are verifiable. A proposition can be verified only if it can be tested against a standard of truth. Putting a proposition up against a standard of truth means taking the chance that the statement can be falsified. Thus, scientific propositions must have the potential to be falsified. This philosophy of scientific inquiry is called "falsificationism."

For the most part, statements that qualify as scientific propositions are falsifiable. They are either mathematical proofs, which can be falsified by showing a flaw in their internal logic, or else hypotheses about what we observe in the world, which can be falsified through careful observations and experiments.

According to that scheme, a belief that cannot be falsified either by logic or by evidence is nothing but dogma. Dogmatic beliefs cannot be falsified, but that is only because you hold onto your dogma regardless of any arguments that can be raised against it.

Reasonable beliefs should not be false, of course, but they should be subject to testing against logic or observation. To put the case for falsificationism another way, one would say that any proposition that cannot be falsified is by the same token a proposition that cannot be verified.

If you hold onto a belief so dogmatically that no evidence could change your mind, then that belief is not falsifiable. Nonfalsifiable dogma is the worst sort of belief. Reasonable people can settle differences of opinion regarding falsifiable statements. Not so with dogma. If that is the case, then scientific argument becomes pointless. That is why scientists prefer to deal in propositions that are falsifiable.

However, not all scientific beliefs are falsifiable. A few key beliefs, called paradigms by Thomas Kuhn,[11] and which I will call "frameworks of interpretation," are so fundamental to how scientists view their subject that they are almost beyond question. For example, Darwin's theory of evolution is a fundamental framework of interpretation in biology. Biologists no longer ask *whether* Darwinian evolution can explain phenomena. Instead, they talk about *how* the theory can be adapted to provide explanations.

A framework of interpretation cannot be falsified. However, many frameworks suffer from anomalies. In evolution, for example, some phenomena, such as a peacock's large tail, would appear to reduce survivability. To address that anomaly, biologists have suggested that the large tail signals strength and attracts potential mates, thereby actually tending to increase the survivability of that characteristic.

The difference between a falsifiable proposition and an interpretive framework is that it takes only one anomaly to

[11] Thomas S. Kuhn, *The Structure of Scientific Revolutions*, 1st ed. (Chicago: University of Chicago Press, 1962).

reject a falsifiable proposition. A single clear-cut logical flaw serves to falsify a logical proposition or mathematical proof. A single conclusive experiment serves to falsify an empirical hypothesis. However, a single anomaly does not lead someone to abandon an interpretive framework. (Keep that in mind the next time you see someone claim that "this one chart" provides definitive proof for or against a particular economic viewpoint.) An anomaly makes scientists uneasy, but they look for ways to address the anomaly without abandoning their interpretive framework.

Up to a point, scientists will stick with an interpretive framework in spite of anomalies. However, if enough anomalies accumulate that scientists become uncomfortable with a framework, and they find that an alternative framework addresses the anomalies and is compatible with existing knowledge, then they will switch to the new framework. That switch is what Kuhn calls a scientific revolution.

In general, I shy away from using the term "social science," because I do not think that economists can aspire to the same level of falsifiability as physicists. I believe that the difference between social science and natural science boils down to this:

In natural science, there are relatively many falsifiable propositions and relatively few attractive interpretive frameworks. In the social sciences, there are relatively many attractive interpretive frameworks and relatively few falsifiable propositions.

The reason that there are relatively few falsifiable propositions in the context of social phenomena is that many causal factors exist, and decisive experiments are rarely possible. Social phenomena are characterized by high causal density, to borrow a term from James Manzi.[12]

As a result, economics is closer to history than to physics. If a historian wants to examine the causes of the decline of Rome, or the decline of empires in general, he or she will provide an interpretive framework. That framework cannot be falsified, but readers can compare it with other frameworks and make judgments about its plausibility.

For example, consider the phenomenon of the comparative salaries of men and women. Economists interpret salaries using the framework of human capital. That is, workers bring to the market different levels of ability, training, and experience, and those attributes determine what they are able to earn. Sociologists use a framework that emphasizes group

---

[12] See James Manzi, *Uncontrolled: The Surprising Payoff of Trial-and-Error for Business, Politics, and Society* (New York: Basic Books, 2012).

identity, status, and power, with men the more dominant group and women the more oppressed group.

If a study were to suggest that women earn less than men, even when controlling for years of education and other indicators of human capital, then that would be an anomaly for the economists. If a study were to suggest that most of the lowest-paying occupations are occupied predominantly by men, then that would be an anomaly for the sociologists. However, such observations will not prove decisive. By invoking other factors to explain anomalous results, each side can remain unmoved. Economists will not abandon their human capital framework, nor will sociologists abandon their group-status framework.

What economists call "models" are interpretive frameworks. They are presented mathematically, with proofs that connect initial assumptions to ultimate predictions. However, the predictions are not falsifiable. The models' predictions hold only when other things are equal, and other things are never equal.

For example, consider the very common equation $Y = f(K,L)$, which says that output is a function of the amount of capital and the amount of labor. One obvious prediction is that more of either factor will tend to increase output.

That production function is used to interpret data in various contexts, including making comparisons of labor productivity.

For example, suppose that Alan's lawn service can mow more lawns per worker than Bob's lawn service. The first variable that an economist will look for to explain the difference is the number of lawn-mowing machines per worker at each firm. If Alan's service does not use more lawn-mowing machines per worker than Bob's, then the economist will look at the quality of the mowing machines at the two firms. If that does not explain the difference, then the economist will fall back on "better management" or some other factor. The less closely that the explanation can be tied to capital, the more anomalous the result will be.

Economists actually try to use the production function to explain productivity differences between entire countries or to explain the historical path of productivity within a country. However, that approach requires taking a weighted average of many different types of outputs and treating the weighted average as if it were a single type of output. Similarly, economists must construct measures of aggregate capital and aggregate labor by taking weighted averages of many different types of each. Many other factors affect aggregate productivity, including endowments of natural resources, government policies, and the diffusion of knowledge. Not surprisingly, in empirical studies, many anomalies can and do crop up, so that the issue of what causes productivity to differ across countries or to change over time remains highly controversial.

Another challenge for economics is that the economy evolves. Consider some of the factors in the relationships between aggregate output, total labor input, and total capital input. Imagine trying to compare the U.S. economy today with that of 50 years ago. We have to take into account major changes, including the following:

- Many fewer people are in the labor force with less than a high school education, and many more people have at least some college education.

- The share of output in agriculture and manufacturing has fallen, whereas the share of output that consists of services has risen.

- Some outputs today, such as smartphones and heart transplant surgeries, cannot be compared with outputs of 50 years ago.

- The share of workers directly involved in production has fallen. The share of workers who are developing organizational capacity has risen.

- The share of computers in total capital has been rising. The cost of this particular type of capital equipment has plummeted sharply, and its characteristics have changed radically, making it difficult to measure reliably how the value of investment in computers has changed over time.

The economy also evolves as new business models, new production processes, and new institutions emerge to solve problems. The "market failures" identified in economic models are only a small fraction of the imperfections that exist at any one time in the economy. Businesses and other organizations are constantly working on solutions to those problems.

Nobel Laureate George Akerlof famously provided an interpretive framework for the used-car market in which high-quality used cars would be kept off the market, because buyers would have to assume, in the absence of other information, that all used cars were "lemons."[13] However, that framework assumes that no market adaptation exists to address the problem. The information problem in the used-car market can be addressed in a variety of ways. For example, mechanics can inspect used cars before consumers purchase them. Sellers can offer warranties on the cars. Decades after Akerlof's article was published, a national used-car dealer called CarMax emerged with a business model based on a reputation for selling high-quality used cars. Other services emerged to make the repair and service records of used cars transparent to buyers.

[13] George A. Akerlof, "The Market for 'Lemons': Quality Uncertainty and the Market Mechanism," *Quarterly Journal of Economics* 84, no. 3 (1970): 488–500.

Markets also adapt in response to our attempts to regulate them. For example, economists have pointed out that the way in which physicians are compensated in the United States, with billing based on procedures, distorts the incentives of doctors so that they tend to perform too many procedures that have high costs and low benefits. However, if that system were changed so that doctors were compensated only according to the number of patients that they see, then we would likely have the opposite problem: to bill for as many patients as possible, doctors would try to avoid doing time-consuming procedures. If doctors were compensated on the basis of patient outcomes, then they would select patients who were likely to have good outcomes, avoiding some of the most difficult patients.

Because of causal density and evolution, economists cannot be certain of the reliability of our assumptions. Thus, any interpretive framework may be inappropriate, depending on circumstances.

Economic models contain many unverifiable assumptions in a context in which plausible alternatives exist. Consequently, when we observe, say, contrary to the expectations derived from a model, a decrease in the price of milk, or an increase in the overall unemployment rate, we do not know which of many assumptions was mistaken or which of many alternative explanations accounts for the data.

In physics or chemistry, the number of unverifiable assumptions and alternative models is whittled down through the process of experimental verification. In economics, because controlled experiments are not feasible, such whittling down cannot take place. A particular equation or set of equations becomes popular in the modern economic literature because economists find it interesting or tractable. But it does not have anything like the experimental support that exists for equations in physics or chemistry.

Economists who employ models think of themselves as "doing science," meaning that they are generating falsifiable propositions. However, in practice, they rarely reject their preferred models. Instead, they explain away anomalous observations. In that sense, they are really using their preferred models as interpretive frameworks.

Even though interpretive frameworks are not falsifiable, that would not matter if the interpretations were never problematic. However, all interpretive frameworks suffer from anomalies, that is, from phenomena that do not easily fit into the framework. Consequently, conflicts between interpretive frameworks are very difficult to resolve. As we saw with male–female pay differentials viewed using the economist's or the sociologist's framework, each side can point to anomalies on the other. What is unfair is to treat the other person's model as falsifiable, unable to survive even a single anomaly, while you privilege your preferred model by explaining away any number of anomalies. Unfortunately, that sort of asymmetry pervades arguments among economists.

In short, I believe that it is useful to think of economists as constructing interpretive frameworks. Those frameworks are fragile, in that there are almost always anomalies—observations that are difficult to interpret using the framework. Popularity of a framework is not necessarily a sign of its strength. If a few leading professors get behind a particular framework and pass it on through their graduate students, then that framework can dominate the academic journals without being demonstrably superior to other frameworks.[14]

We need to be reasonable in acknowledging the anomalies of our preferred frameworks, and we should be restrained in rejecting others' frameworks outright on the basis of one or two anomalies. In choosing which frameworks to endorse, we should seek truth without ultimately finding it. Avoid wallowing in confirmation bias.

[14] I attempt to describe the process of adopting frameworks in macroeconomics in my essay "Memoirs of a Would-Be Macroeconomist," 2013, http://arnoldkling .com/essays/papers/macromemoir.pdf.

Economists do not deal with a subject that offers clear-cut tests of theories. We have to use judgment in deciding which interpretive frameworks to adopt. That does not mean that you should abandon the attempt to reason carefully and rely on simple intuition. Intuition uninformed by any economic framework is at least as flawed as are the frameworks taught in economics courses.

However, you should be wary of economists who claim scientific certainty. President Harry Truman, weary of economists who say, "On the one hand . . . On the other," reportedly pleaded for a one-handed economist. That would be asking for trouble.

Machine as Metaphor

During [Sigmund] Freud's university years (the late 1870s and early 1880s), young enthusiasts in the fuzzier disciplines, such as psychology, liked to borrow terminology from the more rigorous and established field of mechanical physics. The borrowed terms became, in fact, metaphor; and metaphor, like a shrewd servant, has a way of ruling its master. Thus, Freud wound up with the idea that libido or sexual "energy," as he called it, is a pressure that builds up within a closed system to the point where it demands release, as in a steam engine:

Over the past twenty years . . . neurophysiologists have begun to study the actual workings of the brain and central nervous system. These investigators find no buildups of "pressure" or "energy," sexual or otherwise, for the simple reason that the central nervous system is not analogous to an engine. They regard it as more like an electronic circuit, such as a computer or a telephone system.[15]

—Tom Wolfe, "The Boiler Room and the Computer"

Like psychologists, economists were taken with mechanical metaphors, particularly in the aftermath of World War II. Uppermost in their minds were mass-produced machines, such as the T-34 tanks that the Soviet Union used to turn the tide in its struggle against Nazi Germany. Postwar economists naturally thought of an economic problem consisting of allocating key resources, such as steel and oil, among alternative uses, primarily aircraft, warships, and battle tanks.

The graduate program in economics at MIT was at first heavily funded by the U.S. Department of Defense, as

[15] Tom Wolfe, "The Boiler Room and the Computer," in *Mauve Gloves and Madmen, Clutter and Vine: And Other Stories, Sketches, and Essays* (New York: Farrar, Straus and Giroux, 1976).

World War II seemed to show the importance of combining economics with engineering. That combination was particularly useful for addressing problems of constrained optimization. That is, given a fixed capacity to produce, say, steel and rubber tires, what is the optimal quantity of tanks and airplanes to manufacture?

Constrained optimization became a trademark of postwar economic theory. MIT economists modeled both the individual consumer and the individual firm as solving constrained optimization problems. There was even a brief attempt to model all economic policy as solving a constrained optimization problem using a "social welfare function," which would substitute society's values for market prices. MIT and the economics profession as a whole developed confidence that with modeling, mathematics, and statistical information, they could fine-tune the economic machine.

The MIT revolution was led by Paul Samuelson, who in 1970 became the first American to win the Nobel Prize in Economics, and whose textbook dominated the market in the 1950s and 1960s and serves as the template for popular current textbooks.[16]

---

[16] For a fascinating look at Samuelson and the development of postwar economics, I recommend the essays collected in E. Roy Weintraub, *MIT and the Transformation of American Economics* (Durham, NC: Duke University Press, 2014).

Samuelson and his successors taught that the economic machine had a gas pedal that could be used to avoid economic slowdowns. That device was "aggregate demand," which could be increased by the government's printing money, running a budget deficit, or both. In this economic subfield, known as macroeconomics, the concept of specialization is forgotten entirely. Instead, economists employ an interpretive framework in which every worker performs the same job, toiling in one big factory that produces a homogeneous output. Macroeconomics replaces specialization with that GDP factory.

Fifty years ago, those researchers who were not seduced by Freudian metaphors were likely to be enamored of B.F. Skinner, who taught that human behavior could be interpreted as if we were machines that respond predictably to past experiences of pleasure or pain. However, today, many researchers prefer the interpretive framework of evolutionary psychology. They see the human brain as being endowed with capabilities that evolved in the era of hunting and gathering but that can be adapted to very different environments. Both individual behavior and cultural norms respond to more than just the stimuli of reward and punishment.

Although psychology has moved on, the discipline of economics has remained stuck in its mechanistic metaphors. As a result, economists engage in an ultimately futile attempt to apply mathematical methods that are analogous to those used to measure a tank's speed, firepower, and armor. Economists have yet to incorporate metaphors that pertain to the computer or communication networks. They have not come to terms with the reality that an economic system is much more complex than a T-34 tank.

Computer networks, which today offer a powerful metaphor for thinking about the brain or human society, were not around in that key period in the history of economic thought. Until the mid-1970s, the only computers were mainframes, referred to as "big iron." Far larger than today's computing devices, and yet less powerful, computers were classified as heavy equipment. Owning a single mainframe required a massive investment. In the private sector, only the largest businesses could afford them, and only a handful of firms, primarily IBM, could supply them.

Managers thought of mainframe computers as akin to mechanical calculators. Rather than working on general, multipurpose software, most people who wrote computer code were programming the machine to perform a specific calculation.

The advent of the personal computer in the late 1970s and early 1980s brought software to prominence, exemplified by Microsoft. Subsequently, the emergence of the public Internet in the 1990s demonstrated the significance of decentralized networks offering specialized sources of content and connection.

I have come to see software and Internet resources as useful metaphors for the market economy. In my view, it is better to think of the economy in relation to the Internet than in relation to a T-34 tank. A tank performs only a few functions. It is deliberately designed by a small group of engineers. It can be understood and evaluated using a few simple measurements, such as speed, armor thickness, and gun capacity. In contrast, the services available on the Internet perform myriad functions. The resources on the Internet, and the patterns of specialization and trade in the market, emerge from the actions of countless individuals, not from the minds of a few designers. And the factors that affect the value of market production or Internet resources are many, complex, and not all quantifiable.

The "hardware" of the economy consists of its physical resources and physical outputs. However, as with computers, economic "software" is at least as important. Most of the world's wealth is intangible. It consists of our individual and collective knowledge. We know how to transform apparently useless gunk, called oil, into energy. We know how to transform an apparently inert element, called silicon, into computer chips that enable us to process information and to communicate more efficiently. As consumers, we know how to work with complex equipment, such as automobiles and cell phones. As workers, we have great stores of industry-specific and task-specific know-how.

Most of the world's economic backwardness also comes from intangible factors. Where widespread poverty exists, it can be traced to bad governance, violent conflict, counterproductive social norms, and poor education.[17]

Samuelson and his successors created a modern economic orthodoxy that is flawed in several important ways. As we have seen, the engineering approach is best suited to tangible, quantifiable elements, such as the number of hours worked in factories or the number of machines in use. However, economic reality is more subtle and complex.

The MIT-influenced approach that dominates the economics profession treats individual markets and the economy as a whole as if they were simple machines. It embodies a view that economic behavior can be analyzed and predicted on the basis of mathematical equations. The economist plays a role analogous to that of a mechanical engineer, using models and equations to suggest ways for policymakers to make markets operate more efficiently.

[17] For a longer treatment of the importance of intangibles in the economy, see Arnold Kling and Nick Schulz, *Invisible Wealth: The Hidden Story of How Markets Work* (New York: Encounter Books, 2009).

However, economic models of markets are not as powerful as the engineer's model of a machine. Economists' mathematical modeling fails to come to terms with the complexity of economic phenomena. In the real world, too many factors have to be left out of the mathematical models.

Defenders of the modern orthodoxy will argue that the use of mathematics is a way to force economists to keep track of their assumptions. Formal models make assumptions explicit, rather than hiding them. Mathematical derivations demonstrate how the assumptions interact.

The use of mathematics helps verify the connection between assumptions and conclusions, but it does not guarantee that we are making good choices in our assumptions. On the contrary, we often make very bad assumptions, because better assumptions would be too difficult to handle mathematically. Thus, we use "two-by-two" models of international trade, when the reality consists of much more complex forms of specialization. We model "expectations" as a set of identical beliefs held by everyone in the economy, when in fact differences exist among people with regard to information and expectations. We take market imperfections as given, rather than consider how enterprises and institutions might evolve to address current problems.

One example of dubious analysis based on mathematics concerns the question of how retired people should allocate their assets between annuities and ordinary savings. For example, if you have $300,000 in savings, you could use it to obtain an annuity from an insurance company that will pay you, say, $30,000 a year for as long as you live. Instead, suppose that you gradually spend from the savings that you have. In that case, if you live exceptionally long, you face the risk of outliving your savings.

An extensive literature using mathematical modeling says that most or all of retiree savings should be converted to annuities. Economists have even suggested that because few people use annuities, it might be appropriate to force them to do so. For example, Davidoff, Brown, and Diamond write:

> The near absence of voluntary annuitization is puzzling in the face of theoretical results that suggest large benefits to annuitization. While incomplete annuity markets may render annuitization of a large fraction of wealth suboptimal, our simulation results show that this is not the case even in a habit-based model that intentionally leads to a severe mismatch between desired consumption and the single payout trajectory provided by an incomplete annuity

market. These results suggest that lack of annuity demand may arise from behavioral considerations, and that some mandatory annuitization may be welfare increasing.[18]

Knowing of that literature, I had always inferred that annuitization was a good idea, until I observed close relatives reach retirement age. Then, when they asked me for financial advice, I noticed the following considerations:

1. As people reach their later years, their financial needs are dominated by health issues. That means that consumption needs are not smooth. On the contrary, the elderly can face sudden increases in the cost of dealing with disabilities (moving to assisted-living facilities, or requiring a home health aide) and a steady decline in non-health-related spending (less travel and entertainment).

2. A lot of scope for insurance exists within a family. If one spouse lives an exceptionally long time, that spouse can be supported by savings left over from the spouse

---

[18] Thomas Davidoff, Jeffrey R. Brown, and Peter A. Diamond, "Annuities and Individual Welfare," *American Economic Review* 95, no. 5 (2005): 1589.

who died earlier. Alternatively, a long-lived parent can be supported by children.

3. If you wind up spending the last few years of your life in a nursing home, then you are not better off for having an annuity with nothing to spend it on.

In principle, mathematical models can be adapted to take into account real-world complications. In practice, however, economists tend to draw strong conclusions from simple models.

When it comes to the financial sector, mathematics has served economists mainly as a blindfold. Engineering models are poorly suited to articulating the role of financial intermediation in the economy:

- In the engineering model, the essence of economic activity is turning resources into output. However, there is no tangible output from the financial sector to quantify.

- The engineering approach divides into "partial equilibrium," which looks at the behavior of a single market, and "general equilibrium," which looks at the interaction among all markets. The financial sector is important for the way in which it interacts with other sectors, so that it is not well understood using a partial equilibrium approach. However, most general equilibrium models are posed as mathematical problems that can be solved without any financial sector at all.

In his recent book *Foolproof*, financial journalist Greg Ip says of economic policy analysts:

> Philosophically, they fall into two schools of thought. One, which I call the engineers, seeks to use the maximum of our knowledge and ability to solve problems and make the world safer and more stable; the other, which I call the ecologists, regards such experts with suspicion, because given the complexity and adaptability of people and the environment, they will always have unintended consequences that may be worse than the problem we are trying to solve.[19]

I fall on the ecologist side of this divide. Although an engineer thinks of machines as having stable, predictable properties, an ecologist thinks of an evolving, adapting system.

The engineering approach requires a presumption that someone is standing outside the economy—an economic

---

[19] Greg Ip, *Foolproof: Why Safety Can Be Dangerous and How Danger Makes Us Safe* (New York: Little, Brown and Company, 2015), p. 19.

policy adviser—who, with the aid of simple models and equations, clearly sees what it would take to achieve outcomes that
are superior to those that would emerge without government
intervention. The engineers argue, quite reasonably, that we
should not interpret market outcomes as perfect or ideal.
However, they implicitly assume, much less reasonably, that
the political process aided by economic models, will succeed
in correcting the flaws in markets. Moreover, they assume that
individuals and organizations acting in the context of markets
will be unable to adapt to solve the problems that arise.

There are several fundamental concerns with the presumption of a wise, benevolent policy process. It treats the knowledge embedded in an economist's simplified model as though
it were complete knowledge. It ignores the ways that markets
might adapt to solve problems. And it presumes that when
the political process goes to work on problems, it arrives at
solutions flawlessly.

Economists talk about "market imperfections" or "market
failure." However, economic models are themselves imperfect
and capable of failure. If you ask different economic experts to
predict the effect of a change in health insurance regulation
or an increase in the corporate income tax rate, you will get
different answers. The answer that appears to have the stron-
gest support may turn out to be incorrect in practice.

As outsiders, economists see some of the conditions in a market, but they omit other factors. In that regard, economists are no different from other outsiders. To the extent that there are outsiders who see a flaw in how the market serves consumers, those outsiders have the option of starting a business to address the problem. That is what entrepreneurs do all the time, and they are the main engine of economic progress.

However, entrepreneurs are often mistaken, and new businesses often fail. By the same token, economists and policymakers are also capable of making errors. What we should be comparing is not the existing market configuration with an ideal based on a simple model but the market *process* of error correction with the political *process* of error correction.

My skepticism of mechanistic, mathematical modeling leads me to reject the implicit assumption of a nearly omniscient economic adviser. I will return to this subject in the section on policy in practice.

Instructions and Incentives

At Gian-Tony's, an Italian restaurant in Saint Louis, Missouri, my old hometown, the owner, Tony Cataranicchia, is responsible for coordinating the specialization of work. He will instruct the waiters and other service staff. He will help oversee the kitchen workers, as the food preparation process is divided up. One assistant will be told to cut vegetables, another will prepare soup, another will make pasta, and so on.

In society as a whole, however, no one owner is dividing up work and assigning tasks. How can specialization be coordinated? How are production processes divided into tasks, and who designates which people do which tasks?

Before the Industrial Revolution, most people worked the land, either as individual farmers struggling to achieve subsistence or as servants to a lord or emperor. Apart from fieldwork, many societies assigned roles to their members according to custom. Your father's occupation became your occupation. Occupations might be indicated by the family name, such as Baker or Smith (metalworker). In India, the caste system was a detailed, rigid social order that assigned different roles to people at birth.

Within an individual business, like Gian-Tony's, specialization is coordinated by instructions. However, specialization *among* firms is not centrally directed. Instead, specialization emerges from individual decisions that are coordinated by prices and profits.

Nobody ordered the founders of Gian-Tony's to start a restaurant specializing in southern Italian cuisine. Instead, they took an entrepreneurial risk, based on their assessment of their own skills, the potential customer base, and the projected cost of operations.

Nobody instructed a farmer to grow tomatoes for the restaurant. Nobody was ordered to produce veal. Instead, the system of incentives created by prices serves to coordinate the supply of tomatoes, veal, and other ingredients.

What instructions do within a firm is accomplished by prices in the market. That is, the price system acts as a coordination mechanism.

When tomato prices are high, farmers will offer more tomatoes for sale and buyers will cut back on tomato purchases. When prices are low, the opposite happens. In that way, prices serve to guide the amount of specialization in producing tomatoes or other goods.

Prices serve as signals to guide consumers and business owners. A high price for a good signals that it is scarce. Consumers may wish to substitute other goods. Businesses that use that good need to conserve it. Businesses that can supply that good or that can come up with a substitute can profit by expanding production.

What determines which decisions are made within a firm and which decisions are guided by the price system? In other words, what determines the boundaries of a firm? This issue has drawn the interest of many economists.[20]

Think of the firm as a team in which the output of any one individual is difficult to value.[21] Consider a computer

[20] Two examples are the Nobel laureates Ronald Coase and Oliver Williamson.

[21] See Armen A. Alchian and Harold Demsetz, "Production, Information Costs, and Economic Organization," *American Economic Review* 62, no. 5 (1972): 777–95.

programmer working on part of a bank's software system. No one can state precisely the value to the bank of the particular section of code that the programmer works on. All that we know is that the bank cannot pay programmers too much, or else it would be unable to make a profit. And it cannot pay programmers too little, or they would choose to work elsewhere.

If it is possible to attach a precise value to a particular segment of work, then it is possible for that work to be broken out of the firm and outsourced to the market. Thus, if a bank can assign a precise value to a particular software system, it has the option of contracting with an outside firm to build the software for an agreed-upon price.

In short, when the value of different tasks can be isolated, specialization will tend to take place between firms, coordinated by the price system. When the value of a particular task is difficult to measure, because its value varies a great deal depending on how it is combined with other tasks, specialization will tend to take place within a firm, governed by instructions.

There are other important issues in trying to measure value. One of the most important concepts in economics is "opportunity cost." The opportunity cost of a good is the value of the best thing that must be given up to obtain that good. For example, if you spend an hour playing a video game, you might say that the opportunity cost is the value to you of your next-best alternative, which might have been watching a television program, chatting with a friend, or hiking to a lake.

Opportunity cost depends on how you might prefer to use your time or your wealth. It necessarily has a subjective component. Moreover, every step in the production process incurs opportunity cost, which means that individual subjective elements are deeply embedded in the cost of every good and service.

Under a market system, prices reflect values at the margin. Suppose that in a small town, 100 gallons of milk are consumed in a day. The next gallon of milk, or the 101st gallon, is what economists would term the marginal gallon of milk. For consumers, the value of the marginal gallon of milk has to be at least as high as the price, or else the price would have to be reduced in order to induce a consumer to purchase it. For producers, the price has to be at least as high as the cost of providing the next gallon of milk (including the opportunity costs embedded in all stages of production), or else the price would have to be increased in order to induce producers to supply it. The actual price should tend to settle at the level that is neither too high for the marginal consumer nor too low for the marginal producer.

Individuals respond to the incentives created by the price system. The surgeon who is very fast at mowing lawns sees nonetheless that the price system gives her an incentive to stick to surgery. By performing one surgery, she can earn enough to pay for a summer's worth of lawn service.

Profits are another important incentive. When farmers see higher profits in soybeans than in corn, some corn growers will switch to growing soybeans. In that way, profits help direct the economy's resources to the uses that are most desired by consumers.

Profits also provide an incentive for ambitious entrepreneurs to start businesses that address weaknesses in the existing market, providing better goods and services at lower costs. Entrepreneurs profit when they successfully implement ideas for products that give consumers more satisfaction, lower prices, or both.

Note that profit as normally reported by businesses differs from profit as defined by economists. Suppose that instead of playing baseball one summer, superstar Mike Trout were to run a business that reported $100,000 in profit. Because his opportunity cost is a multimillion dollar salary, his economic profit is negative, the reported $100,000 profit notwithstanding.

Equally important, "profit" as conventionally reported includes compensation to investors who supplied the funds needed for the business to get off the ground and to obtain expensive equipment. Suppose that I develop an app myself and get $100,000 in revenue in the first year. Meanwhile, someone else raises $500,000 in venture funding and pays programmers $500,000 to develop an app that earns $700,000 in revenue in the first year. That second firm will report $200,000 in profit, even though some of that "profit" is compensation to the investors for the risk and opportunity cost they incurred with their investment.

Patterns of specialization and trade evolve because of two mechanisms: substitution and innovation. Substitution takes place on the basis of existing technology. Innovation represents the successful implementation of new methods of production or new means of satisfying consumer wants.

Both consumers and producers engage in substitution. When corn becomes more expensive than wheat, consumers will respond to the price change by buying fewer corn-based products and more wheat-based products. Meanwhile, farmers will shift some production from wheat to corn. Because of those substitution responses, the price system avoids possible shortages or surpluses and instead achieves balance between supply and demand. When a shortage might otherwise appear, a rise in the price induces changes in behavior that tend to eliminate the shortage. When a surplus might otherwise appear, a fall in the price induces behavior that works to prevent that surplus.

Ironically, one important factor leading to changes in patterns of specialization and trade is market imperfections.

After half a century in which MIT economics has penetrated our culture, many educated people automatically think that when markets produce bad outcomes, the only solution is some government intervention. In fact, most of the solutions to market imperfections are launched by private entrepreneurs, who identify shortcomings of existing products and services and who start new businesses or launch new ideas within existing businesses in order to address those shortcomings.

The process of innovation has three components. First is "experimentation," in which a business tries a new product or service or a new method of production. Second is "evaluation," where the business managers determine whether the new idea is successful or not. Third is "evolution," in which successful business models are expanded, and failed business models are discarded.

Profits play a key role in that process. The prospect of profits encourages entrepreneurs to attempt experiments. Those experiments are evaluated on the basis of whether or not they indeed achieve profits. The businesses that survive the evolutionary process are the profitable ones, and unprofitable businesses close down.

Profits are a measure of the sustainability of patterns of specialization. When a business that participates in a pattern of specialization earns a profit, the value of its output is greater than the cost of its inputs. That outcome indicates that the business is making a positive contribution to consumer well-being.

Sustainability depends on context. Just because a business made a positive contribution yesterday does not guarantee that it will do so today. Perhaps an important input becomes more expensive, which is an indication that it needs to be conserved for use elsewhere. Perhaps the price that the firm can charge for output has fallen, which is an indication that consumer tastes have shifted or that a competing firm has developed a more efficient way of providing similar output. In either case, profits go away, and that is a signal that the firm must improve its efficiency or else eventually go out of business.

Under a market system, entrepreneurs constantly test new ideas that rearrange patterns of specialization. New arrangements that earn profits survive. Both new arrangements and old arrangements that fail to earn profits fall by the wayside. In that way, the market continually evolves toward greater efficiency, meaning satisfying human needs at less cost.

We tend to want to discuss cost as if it were an objective concept, intrinsic to the output being produced. After all, the resources used by a business, including labor time, have prices attached to them. In that sense, it seems as if the cost of output can be calculated objectively, by adding up the value of all of the inputs. However, in a world of specialization, the search for a straightforward, objective measure of cost is doomed to fail.

As we look more deeply, we see that the cost of output depends on market conditions and individual judgments that are not intrinsic to what is being produced. Input prices reflect opportunity costs. The price of an input is the value of that input in its next-best alternative use. But we have no objective way of determining the best alternative use for inputs, especially the input of each worker's time and effort. The value of an input depends on what alternatives are available, on people's tastes, and on the state of knowledge. Those factors are not directly observable, and they are constantly changing.

Because of the importance of unobservable factors in determining value and cost, a distant observer is not in a position to evaluate economic performance with certainty. For example, suppose we want to compare the efficiency of two methods of growing corn. If one method uses less of every input, then it is clearly more efficient. However, if one method uses more water but requires less of the farmer's time, then we cannot tell which method is more efficient. It depends on how farmers value their time relative to the cost of water.

Choices and Commands

An economy as a whole may be coordinated by centralized commands or by decentralized choices made in response to the incentives created by prices and profits. With centralization, a single body of decisionmakers is responsible for coordination. With decentralization, no one entity is in charge; instead, the impersonal price and profit mechanism gives direction to the economy.

Suppose we think of the ruler of a society making an either-or decision using those methods. We would have four possibilities:

	Do not use the price system	Use the price system
Do not use commands	Utopian socialism	Pure market economy
Use commands	Command economy	Mixed system

Try to imagine specialization coordinated with neither commands nor market prices. Instead, individuals decide for themselves what role to play in the production process in order to satisfy people's wants. In the words of Karl Marx, "From each according to his abilities, to each according to his needs." That is the ideal of utopian socialism. Note that neither Marx nor other utopian socialists spelled out how that ideal was supposed to work.

Utopian socialists tend to underestimate the complexity of the challenge of coordinating the millions of tasks that are divided up in a specialized economy. For example, in 2009, philosopher G. A. Cohen wrote a book titled *Why Not Socialism?*[22] Cohen used the metaphor of a camping trip as a model for utopian socialism.

On a camping trip, we might expect people to organize easily to perform the necessary tasks to set up camp and to cook meals. No one needs price incentives to put up a tent, start a fire, or peel potatoes. Neither does anyone need to be commanded to do those things.

However, it is important to understand why a camping expedition is an inappropriate metaphor for the economy as a whole:

- On a camping trip, we deliberately choose to restrict our consumption to a more primitive level than what

[22] G. A. Cohen, *Why Not Socialism?* (Princeton, NJ: Princeton University Press, 2009).

we ordinarily prefer. Although we are camping, we do not expect to be served Thai food, to watch our favorite sport on television, or to have a tooth cavity filled. We can do without such luxuries for a few days, until we return home.

- On a camping trip, there are relatively few people. Thus, the scope for specialization is limited.

- But most important of all, we begin the camping trip with a set of goods that requires millions of tasks to have been performed elsewhere, by people not on the trip. Where did our clothes come from? The tent? The food and utensils that we brought along? And so on.

A camping trip is a misleading metaphor for an economy, because we arrive at our campsite already in possession of a wealth of goods. On the trip itself, only a small amount of production takes place relative to the rich endowment with which we start. It is that prior production that requires extensive coordination, and such extensive coordination requires either a price system or commands.

In the world of utopian socialism, people would choose pleasant jobs and avoid unpleasant ones. There would be plenty of singer-guitarists, actors, and tennis players, but few chicken farmers, oil well operators, or sanitation workers.

In the absence of commands or prices, nothing complex would be produced. Even making an appliance as mundane as a toaster requires many steps and uses material from disparate regions of the world.[23] People cannot spontaneously organize to make a toaster, much less an airplane or a smartphone. Complex production requires both instructions within firms and a coordination mechanism among firms. It cannot take place without either government planning and direction or the market system of prices and profits.

Inside a firm, a pure market economy is as difficult to imagine as utopian socialism. In a pure market economy, all decisions are made in response to prices. If the inside of a firm were run like a market economy, then a construction supervisor would not order workers to pour concrete or hammer nails. Instead, workers would calculate which tasks to perform on the basis of the market prices for each task.

Within a firm, as we have seen, production takes place in teams and individual tasks are difficult to value. As a result, economic activity within a firm requires central planning and organization. However, between firms, coordination takes place through the price system. Complete government control over planning is required only in a pure command economy.

[23] See Thomas Thwaites, *The Toaster Project: Or a Heroic Attempt to Build a Simple Electric Appliance from Scratch* (New York: Princeton Architectural Press, 2011).

A pure command economy is rarely observed, except under conditions of total war. In World War II, the Soviet Union was able to produce sufficient arms, including T-34 tanks, to stall and eventually defeat the Nazi invaders. During that war, a large share of economic activity was directed by government in all of the major fighting nations, including the United States and Great Britain. That is, they acquired about half of the total output, rationed many consumer goods, and fixed prices.

For a few decades after the war, economic planning was in good repute. John Kenneth Galbraith, a Harvard economist who had participated in wartime government regulation of prices, wrote a book titled *The New Industrial State*, in which he argues that entrepreneurship and decentralized markets were quaint myths:

> The enemies of the market are not socialists. . . . [They] are advanced technology, the specialization and organization of men and process that this requires and the resulting commitment of time and capital. These make the market work badly when the need is for greatly enhanced reliability—when planning is essential. The modern large Western corporation and the modern apparatus of socialist planning are variant accommodations to the same need. . . . [Do] not ask that jet aircraft, nuclear power plants or

even the modern automobile in its modern volume be produced by firms that are subject to unfixed prices and unmanaged demand.[24]

In 1967, when Galbraith first published those words, we had experienced 100 years in which the economy had apparently come to be dominated by industrial giants, such as U.S. Steel, General Motors, or Standard Oil. He was writing in the tradition of Progressive thinkers, who since the end of the 19th century had argued that a dramatic increase in the scale of business enterprise had made both the economics of Adam Smith and the weak central government of the U.S. Constitution anachronistic. They saw mass production as requiring organization and planning, and Galbraith was not alone in regarding a command economy as a viable economic system.

However, apart from wartime experiences, extensive government control of the economy has tended to break down. The economic collapse of the Soviet Union in the 1980s is a historical demonstration of the failure of a command economy.

Galbraith's analysis is confounded by more than just the failure of Communism. Most of the large enterprises that

[24] John Kenneth Galbraith, *The New Industrial State* (Boston: Houghton Mifflin, 1967; Princeton, NJ: Princeton University Press, 2015), p. 41.

appeared to dominate the economy when he wrote are now much diminished. The nation's large steel makers disappeared. American automobile manufacturers have struggled to survive. Neither the production of jet aircraft nor the construction of nuclear power plants is important to our economy today. Many contemporary giants, such as Google and Apple, do not resemble the old industrial powerhouses in numbers of employees or investment in plants and equipment. Ingenuity and innovation, rather than organization and planning, are the qualities most often credited for success today.

A Galbraithian corporation should have been nearly immune from the Schumpeterian forces of creative destruction. Its "technostructure" (Galbraith's term for managers and experts) was supposed to minimize the risk of the firm's investments and to ensure control over its environment. Instead, the majority of companies that were in the Dow Jones Industrial Average when Galbraith wrote have disappeared from the ranks of America's leading businesses. As of now, the 30 stocks that make up the Dow include Apple, Microsoft, Nike, Cisco Systems, Home Depot, and at least a dozen other companies that in 1967 either did not exist or were just beginning to grow. The U.S. corporate sector is characterized at least as much by Darwinian competition as by planning.

A command economy faces three major problems. First is an information problem, in which the absence of prices puts central planners at a disadvantage in making production and allocation decisions. Second is an incentive problem. Without prices and profits to act as incentives, it becomes difficult to sustain important social norms, including the work ethic. In actual planned economies, we have seen social morale degenerate while cynicism and corruption spread. Third is a lack-of-innovation problem. Central planners have difficulty generating the progress that in a market economy comes from experimentation, evaluation, and evolution.

Central planners face an information problem. They must decide what goods and services are produced, how they are produced, and who gets what. However, they must do so without the information provided by market prices.[25]

In a command economy, there is no price signal. Instead, planners must make assumptions about the value of outputs and about the technology for converting resources into outputs. Given those assumptions, the mathematical techniques developed by MIT-style economists can be used

---

[25] The information problem is part of a classic discussion in economics known as "the socialist calculation debate." Ludwig von Mises and F. A. Hayek argued for the point made here, which is that without market prices, central planners lack the information necessary to coordinate production effectively.

to compute the values of resources. Economists call those computed values "shadow prices," because they are computed by central planners, not by the market.

Consider a wartime economy, in which planners must decide whether to try to build more ships or more tanks. They must assess the relative usefulness of ships and tanks. For example, they might calculate that they can get the same military value by building one battleship or 250 tanks. They must estimate the amount of various types of inputs, such as labor time and steel, that are needed to produce ships and tanks. Using those estimates, the planners can derive "shadow prices" for labor and steel.

That process works less well in a peacetime economy. Your military chiefs may be able to estimate the relative value of ships and tanks. However, central planners do not know the relative value to consumers of various goods and services.

For example, consider corn flakes and wheat bread. In a market economy, the price system would regulate the supply and demand for those products. If there is a shortage of corn, then the price of corn flakes will rise until consumers reduce their consumption of corn flakes at the margin. Moreover, farmers will see a profit opportunity in switching some acreage from wheat to corn, and their actions will in turn alleviate the corn shortage.

In a command economy, central planners give each family ration coupons for corn flakes and wheat bread. If you were to give a family more ration coupons for corn flakes, then the family would gladly use them. If you were to give a family more ration coupons for wheat bread, then the family would gladly use those. Consumers have no way of signaling to planners that in *relative* terms they would prefer more corn flakes.

Similarly, workers have no way of signaling to central planners that they have untapped skills. It is unlikely that a government agency would have figured out that J. K. Rowling would make an excellent writer of fantasy novels for children or that Steve Jobs would make a creative catalyst for technological innovation.

Midlevel managers in a capitalist economy who see ways to improve the efficiency within their firms can either convince upper management to make changes or leave to start competing firms. In a command economy, such ideas will be implemented only if they happen to come to the attention of top government officials.

Because central planners are not mind readers, they are unable to incorporate the individual's subjective judgments of opportunity cost. Hence, when central planners attribute costs to producing different outputs, they are merely guessing.

A command economy suffers from a lack of competition. Competition helps the price system function. Without any competition, a milk supplier would be free to charge a much higher price than the cost of producing the marginal gallon of milk. If an employer faced no competition for hiring workers, it could pay wages far below the value of what the workers provide.

Competition and reputation are a form of decentralized regulation. If a firm offers shoddy merchandise or engages in deceptive sales practices, its reputation is likely to suffer, and competitors can take away its business. If a firm attempts to exploit workers by imposing harsh working conditions, competing firms can bid away its labor supply.

Competition also disciplines management. If a restaurant is poorly run, it will not provide customers with good value for their money. That will create an opportunity for well-managed competing restaurants to take business away from the poorly run firm.

In short, the price system and competition in a market economy provide information. That information is used to shift resources among different uses, averting surpluses and shortages and guiding inputs to their most efficient use. A command economy lacks that information, and its allocation of resources is only as good as the intuition of the central planners.

Another challenge for a command economy is maintaining social morale in the absence of incentives. Hard work and thrift require self-discipline. In a market economy, self-discipline tends to be rewarded with higher income. Sooner or later, the boss figures out who is working and who is shirking. If the boss cannot figure that out, then sooner or later that boss will be fired. Or if the boss is not fired, then sooner or later a competing firm will make it impossible for the inefficient firm to survive.

In a command economy, it is up to the central planners to decide who to reward and who to punish. If the central planners make mistakes, then there is no correction mechanism. In practice, in centrally planned economies, workers eventually figure out how to "game the system." That is, workers satisfy the stated requirements of the planners while undermining the enterprise in unobservable ways. For example, workers may meet a production quota but with defective goods.

Gaming the system can take even more flagrant forms. In a Soviet-style economy, bribery and corruption tend to be rampant. Ambitious people focus on ingratiating themselves with government officials, whereas in a market economy, the incentive would be to focus on figuring out ways to please customers.

We have seen that within each firm, managers rely on instructions and commands, rather than on prices. That approach creates some of the same problems as in a command economy. That is, within any one firm, workers try to game the system. They try to get the most pay with the least effort. Managers must constantly revise and improve their methods for determining bonuses and other rewards to try to ensure that the incentives in fact lead employees to work harder and more effectively.

Competition among firms means that the firms that come up with the most effective incentive systems and monitoring mechanisms to address gaming are the ones that survive. That in turn helps raise morale in the society overall, since people observe that self-discipline tends to be rewarded more than gaming the system.

A Soviet-style economy is subject to demoralization, as shirking and corruption take over. A market economy can maintain better morale, as long as competition works sufficiently well.

Competition is also important for dynamic efficiency. Dynamic efficiency means sifting through ideas for new production processes and new goods and services in order to adopt those ideas that improve economic performance. Those ideas can be embodied in new firms or attempted by existing businesses. In either case, many new ideas are unsuccessful, and only a few new ideas represent dramatic improvements.

The new ideas that foster dynamic efficiency enter the economy through experimentation, evaluation, and evolution. Profit incentives and competition play crucial roles in that process.

In the absence of competition, most organizations would prefer not to experiment with new ideas. It is more comfortable to stick with old habits. However, if new entrants can compete, then they can test the new ideas that the older organizations are reluctant to employ. Moreover, the threat of new entrants puts pressure on existing organizations to attempt experiments that they would otherwise be reluctant to undertake.

When a new idea is tried, it serves to rearrange the patterns of specialization and trade in the economy. How well does this new pattern work? The answer is indicated by profits and losses. Patterns of specialization and trade that allow the economy to satisfy more consumer desires at lower cost will prove to be profitable. Inferior patterns will incur losses. Thus, profits and losses play a critical role in sifting new ideas, selecting those that are useful, and weeding out those that are not. The profit and loss system is a mechanism for evaluating innovations. Central planners do not have such a mechanism.

Moreover, even if central planners had a method for evaluating innovations, they are not under pressure to discard bad ideas and adopt new ones. Suppose that new software can enable someone else to complete in one hour an engineering design that would take me two weeks. I will perceive that software as a threat to my economic value and status. In a command economy, I may be able to suppress that threat and keep anyone from using the software. In a competitive economy, I cannot do so.

The central planners in a command economy, as in any individual firm or organization, will tend to fear experimentation. People in powerful positions know that their status can be maintained under the status quo. Change represents a threat. They will tend to resist evolution that requires significant change. In contrast, in a market economy the resistance of any individual firm can be rendered moot by the overall force of competition.

In a competitive economy, the incumbents are less able to resist change. Ambitious individuals who are not in high positions at incumbent organizations will see opportunities to get ahead using innovative ideas. They can obtain support from other ambitious innovators and investors and form new firms to challenge the existing enterprises.

Profits and competition will lead to evolution away from inefficient patterns of specialization and trade. Firms that stick with inefficient patterns will incur losses and be forced out of business. The firms that survive will be those that participate in the most efficient patterns of specialization and trade.

In practice, we observe neither a pure command economy nor a pure market economy. In the United States, many government regulations serve the function of commands. Those regulations affect the calculations that consumers and businesses must make. In theory, regulation could improve those calculations by forcing market participants to deal with factors that they otherwise might ignore. However, in practice, regulators are subject to the same pitfalls as the central planners in a hypothetical planned economy. I will return to this issue in the section on policy in practice.

Specialization and Sustainability

It is very hard to be against sustainability. In fact, the less you know about it, the better it sounds.

—Robert M. Solow, "Sustainability: An Economist's Perspective"

Although economists do not know enough to engineer society, they can still correct the intuitions of noneconomists. The issue of sustainability illustrates this point.

What is sustainable in a modern, specialized economy differs from what is sustainable in a hunter-gatherer tribe. On this point, there is alignment between myself and MIT economists, including Nobel Laureate Robert Solow.

As Solow points out in his lecture "Sustainability: An Economist's Perspective," the term "sustainability" is subject to varying interpretations. Depending on which interpretation one chooses, sustainability could be congruent with a market economy, or it could rule out economic activity altogether.[26]

Human economic activity alters the environment. We nurture some species of plants and animals, and we hamper others. We transform plants, animal products, and minerals into different forms. We use chemical reactions that change matter from one form to another. Some of those chemical reactions provide us with energy in useful forms.

Suppose we were to define sustainability as leaving the natural environment exactly as we found it. That definition is appropriate for a society of hunters and gatherers. If you want to hunt and gather sustainably, you cannot kill game or gather plants at a higher rate than they are naturally replenished. However, such a strict definition will not accommodate more advanced economic activity characterized by specialization. Living by such a definition would in fact require that we revert to hunting and gathering.

[26] Robert M. Solow, "Sustainability: An Economist's Perspective," lecture presented at Woods Hole Oceanographic Institution, Woods Hole, MA, June 14, 1991; reprinted in Robert Dorfman and Nancy Dorfman, eds., *Economics of the Environment: Selected Readings* (New York : W. W. Norton, 1993).

In his lecture, Solow disparages a UNESCO document that seemed to espouse such primitivism:

> If you define sustainability as an obligation to leave the world as we found it in detail, I think that's glib but essentially unfeasible. It is, when you think about it, not even desirable. . . . [I]t would mean to do no permanent construction or semi-permanent construction; build no roads; build no dams; build no piers. . . . I doubt that I would feel myself better off if I had found the world exactly as the Iroquois left it.[27]

Instead, Solow offers a definition of sustainability that is more congenial to economists:

> It is an obligation to conduct ourselves so that we leave to the future the option or the capacity to be as well off as we are. . . . Sustainability is an injunction not to satisfy ourselves by impoverishing our successors.[28]

However, this economic definition does not offer clear, precise guidance for how we should deal with any particular resource. Moreover, what we leave to future generations includes more

[27] Ibid., p. 180.
[28] Ibid., p. 181.

than just the natural environment. As Solow puts it, you have to take into account

> the built environment, including productive capacity (plant and equipment) and including technological knowledge.[29]

To our descendants, we leave machinery, transportation equipment, and buildings—what economists call capital. However, we also bequeath what I have been calling the "software" of the economy. We leave a set of institutions, including social norms, rules, and regulations, that have been found conducive to prosperity. We leave a pattern of specialization and trade that satisfies human wants and that is evolving to satisfy them at lower cost. We leave the knowledge that we have accumulated through the process of experimentation, evaluation, and evolution.

Consider what our recent ancestors have left us. The authors of the U.S. Constitution left the United States with a system of government under which new leaders have always taken office peacefully, without coups or revolutions. Scientists and engineers have left us with their know-how. Inventors in the 19th century left us with the railroad and the means

---

[29] Ibid.

for long-distance communication. Inventors in the early 20th century left us with the automobile and the airplane. Inventors in the late 20th century left us with the computer and the Internet. Most important of all, our recent ancestors have left us with the means of living longer and healthier lives, thanks to sanitation and modern medicine.

As economists, we see the market mechanism as serving to measure and promote sustainability. Profits measure sustainability, and the processes of substitution and innovation promote sustainability.

The market measure of sustainability is profit. To earn a profit, a business must transform inputs into output that is more valuable. If a business were to deplete one of its crucial inputs, its cost of production would rise, profits would turn to losses, and the business would have to stop.

The owner of farmland will want to replenish the nutrients in the soil rather than deplete them and be unable to grow crops. People who heat their homes will use the cheapest fuel. If wood becomes more expensive than natural gas, people will switch from burning wood to burning natural gas.

For a business in a market economy, profits come from "doing more with less." Firms compete in an attempt to satisfy the most human wants using the least costly combination of resources. By continually searching for ways to do more with less, the market process of specialization and trade promotes sustainability.

In a market economy, sustainability is assessed using the price system. If two methods for producing a given output exist, the market will select the method that uses the fewest resources *when those resources are valued at market prices.*

For the market to work ideally as a system for promoting sustainability, at least two conditions would have to be satisfied. First, market prices would have to reflect the cost of resources. Second, the issue of intergenerational equity that Solow emphasizes would have to be addressed.

However, market prices reflect costs only when resources are owned and priced. That is not always the case. Consider air quality, for example. Since no one owns the air in Pittsburgh, the market has no means for stopping cars and factories from polluting that air.

Similarly, since no one owns the oceans, the market has no means for stopping overfishing. Since no one owns the atmosphere, the market has no means for ensuring that humans do not use processes that emit too much carbon dioxide.

Sometimes, common resources can be managed well by private organizations. In the case of fish, one approach is for fishermen to get together and agree on quotas and on a mechanism for enforcement. Another approach is to create private fish farms.

Private fish farms alter the incentives for catching fish. The owner of such a fish farm will want to sustain the supply of fish, just as the owner of a herd of cattle will want to sustain the herd.

When market incentives are problematic, the question is not whether market prices are ideal or private solutions are perfect. The question is when should individuals or policy-makers use their own judgment to override the information that market prices give them?

For example, consider the recycling of paper and plastic. To increase the amount of recycling, many local governments subsidize recycling, compel citizens to recycle, or both. However, the market provides the necessary incentive to use resources wisely. That is, an entrepreneur could, in principle, start a business of buying old newspapers or used beverage bottles and selling them for reuse. If the benefit of recycling exceeded the cost, then such recycling could be undertaken at a profit. Instead, we can infer from the necessity to force or subsidize recycling that recycling does not pay. When all costs are accounted for, recycling wastes resources rather than conserving them. Recycling is, in a word, unsustainable.

To start to build a case demonstrating that recycling does not waste resources, one would have to show that there is a flaw in the market pricing of used paper and plastic products. Perhaps the market does not adequately account for the cost of landfills, for example. However, it seems more likely that it is the environmentalists and elected officials who are making erroneous cost calculations. They are overestimating the benefits and underestimating the costs of the recycling system.

Another policy that likely serves to reduce sustainability is the mandate to add ethanol to gasoline. That mandate in turn requires growing more corn to produce ethanol. The intent of the ethanol mandate is to reduce the amount of carbon dioxide emitted by automobiles. However, overall resource use is increased, because of the cost of growing the additional corn. And we cannot be sure that the carbon dioxide emitted by the corn-growing process does not exceed the reduction achieved by the use of ethanol.

Many people believe intuitively that it saves resources to "buy local." Surely, we think, cheese or vegetables from a local farm must save on the energy required for transportation. However, if the grocery store sells cheaper produce that comes from hundreds of miles away, some factor must offset the higher transportation cost. Chances are, the land elsewhere is more suited to growing crops, so that fewer acres are used to produce a given amount of output. The local land might be better used for housing or as wilderness.

Water or other resources may be used more heavily locally than on distant farms. Whenever produce from distant farms is cheaper than locally grown produce, the price system is telling us that "buying local" wastes resources.

One might be skeptical that market prices work to protect the environment, but there is in fact compelling historical evidence that this is the case. Jesse Ausubel, an environmental economist at Rockefeller University, has written an essay that summarizes some of the results of market trends in the use of resources.[30] He writes:

> Since about 1940 American farmers have quintupled corn while using the same or even less land. Corn matters because it towers over other crops, totaling more tons than wheat, soy, rice, and potatoes together . . . .

> The inputs to agriculture have plateaued and then fallen, not just cropland but nitrogen, phosphates, potash, and even water. A recent meta-analysis by Wilhelm Klümper and Matin Qaim of 147 original studies of recent trends in high-yield farming for soy, maize, and cotton, funded by the German government and the European Union, found a 37 percent

[30] Jesse H. Ausubel, "Nature Rebounds," Long Now Foundation Seminar, San Francisco, January 13, 2015, pp. 3–7, http://phe.rockefeller.edu/docs/Nature _Rebounds.pdf.

decline in chemical pesticide use while crop yields rose 22 percent. The story is precision agriculture, in which we use more bits, not more kilowatts or gallons.

When farming becomes more efficient, farmland reverts to wilderness. Ausubel writes:

> Abandonment of marginal agricultural lands in the former Soviet Union and Eastern Europe has released at least 30 million hectares and possibly as much as 60 million hectares to return to nature according to careful studies by geographer Florian Schierhorn and his colleagues. Thirty million hectares is the size of Poland or Italy. The great reversal of land use that I am describing is not only a forecast, it is a present reality in Russia and Poland as well as Pennsylvania and Michigan.

Ausubel points out that the amount of forest is now increasing in many advanced countries. That increase reflects in part the reduction in farm acreage, the use of alternative sources of energy and building materials, and more efficient forest management.

> Foresters refer to a "forest transition" when a nation goes from losing to gaining forested area. France

recorded the first forest transition, about 1830. Since that time French forests have doubled while the French population has also doubled. Forest loss decoupled from population.

Measured by growing stock, the USA enjoyed its forest transition around 1950, and measured by area, about 1990. . . . The thick green cover of New England, Pennsylvania, and New York today would be unrecognizable to Teddy Roosevelt, who knew them as wheat fields, pastures mown by sheep, and hillsides denuded by logging.

There has been an overall increase in plant life on earth. Ausubel writes:

The biosphere on land is getting bigger, year by year, by 2 billion tons or even more. . . . [G]lobal greening is the most important ecological phenomenon on land today.

Ausubel and colleagues find that since 1970, the use of many commodities, such as cadmium and iron ore, has dropped in the United States, in spite of a near doubling of population. Some of that reduction reflects greater efficiency, and some of it reflects the shift in economic activity toward services, as households have become relatively saturated with manufactured products.

Ausubel points out that even as farm output and overall population have increased, use of water in the United States has actually declined since 1970. That change reflects greater efficiency in farming. (Ask your friends who proudly "buy local" whether they know how much water their local farmers use compared with the distant farmers from whom the supermarket imports produce.)

On the energy front, Ausubel notes that car use appears to have peaked. As a result of that and improved efficiency, two economists working in the Obama administration write that "in 2014 Americans used less petroleum than they did in 1997, despite the fact that the economy is nearly 50 percent larger than it was 17 years ago."[31]

On a more pessimistic note, Ausubel points to a significant depletion of edible fish in the world's oceans. He suggests that the solution is fish farming, because the owner of a farm will have an incentive to avoid depleting the fish:

> Fish biomass in intensively exploited fisheries appears to be about one-tenth the level of the fish in those seas a few decades or hundred years ago. . . . If we

---

[31] Brian Deese and Jason Furman, "The Boon of Reduced Oil Consumption," *Washington Post*, June 18, 2015.

want to eat sea life, we need to increase the share we farm and decrease the share we catch.[32]

Generally speaking, in a market economy, the combination of incentives and human ingenuity has permitted the human population to grow with a reduction in the rate of resource use. By selling books in digital format, online retailer Amazon is letting us read more while using less paper; Airbnb is giving us more places to sleep without building hotels; and iTunes is allowing us to listen to more music without manufacturing records. We are not only leaving future generations with more know-how and more tools of production, we are also leaving them with more wilderness, more forest, and more vegetation.

The question of sustainability is this: can we keep doing what we are doing? The market calculates the answer by looking at the profits from specialization and trade. When profits are positive, the market answer is yes. Otherwise, the market answer is no. When your intuition is to dispute that answer, you have to be careful to make sure that you are not the one who is making the miscalculation.

[32] Ausubel, "Nature Rebounds," p. 12.

Trade and Trust

In the 21st century, many of us shop on the Internet. How do I know that the biking gloves I order really have the padding that I want? How do I know that the retailer will send me the gloves that I order? How do I know that the gloves will not be stolen before I receive them?

When you consider those sorts of questions, you realize that our modern market economy is built on layers of trust. For trade to take place, individual beliefs, cultural norms, and formal institutions must be aligned to reinforce such trust.

When we humans lived in small bands of hunter-gatherers, we built trust through repeated interaction. We dealt with the same people, day in and day out. When we encountered a stranger, we reacted with suspicion, and we were prone to engage in violence. Even today, violence and xenophobia have not been expunged from human nature. They have been somewhat repressed by cultural evolution. That cultural evolution is one of the most important ways in which we humans have differentiated ourselves from our chimpanzee ancestors.

Joseph Henrich, an anthropologist, argues that it is not as individuals that humans are distinctively intelligent. Rather, it is our ability to learn from one another and pass our learning on to future generations that makes humans unique. He writes:

> The key to understanding how humans evolved and why we are so different from other animals is to recognize that we are a *cultural species*. Probably over a million years ago, members of our evolutionary lineage began learning from each other in such a way that culture became cumulative. . . . [K]nowledge began to improve and aggregate—by learning from others—so that one generation could build on and hone the skills and know-how gleaned from the previous generation. After several generations, this process produced a sufficiently large and complex toolkit of practices and techniques that individuals, relying on their own ingenuity and personal experience,

could not get anywhere close to figuring out over their lifetime.[33]

One of the advantages of cultural learning is that it permits specialization. Although some animal colonies have specialists, they are genetically programmed. Only humans are able to teach ourselves new specialties.

Henrich writes about the importance of norms as part of cultural learning:

The secret of our species' success resides not in the power of our individual minds, but in the collective brains of our communities. Our *collective brains* arise from the synthesis of our cultural and social natures—from the fact that we readily learn from others (are *cultural*) and can, with the right norms, live in large and widely interconnected groups (are *social*). The striking technologies that characterize our species, from the kayaks and compound bows used by hunter-gatherers to the antibiotics and airplanes of the modern world, emerge not from

[33] Joseph Henrich, *The Secret of Our Success: How Culture Is Driving Human Evolution, Domesticating Our Species, and Making Us Smarter* (Princeton, NJ: Princeton University Press, 2015), p. 3 (emphasis in original).

singular geniuses but from the flow and recombi-
nation of ideas, practices, lucky errors, and chance
insights among interconnected minds and across
generations. . . . [I]nnovation in our species depends
more on our sociality than on our intellect, and the
challenge has always been how to prevent communities from fragmenting and social networks from
dissolving.[34]

For markets to function, our cultural learning has to include
norms for promoting trust. Social scientists have developed a
number of intriguing theories to try to explain how we have
managed to build trust among strangers. Much of that theo-
rizing starts with simple game theory.

In many situations, people can choose either to cooperate or to defect. To cooperate means to obey norms that
are beneficial when everyone follows them but that are not
necessarily in your best interest in the short run. To defect
means to do what is best for you in the short run, even though
there would be adverse consequences if everyone were to act
that way. For example, you might take advantage of a store's
return policy by buying a dress with the intention of wear-
ing it once to a party and then returning it. That behavior

[34] Ibid., pp. 5–6 (emphasis in original).

would be defection, because if everyone did that instead of buying dresses, stores would have to stop allowing customers to return dresses.

One of the main techniques that people use to deter defection is retaliation. We punish people who defect. Economists have noted, however, that in many situations it takes cooperation to punish defectors. Social trust requires people to cooperate in retaliation. You cannot have trust if people defect from punishing defectors!

For a society to remain cohesive, it must implement this basic social rule:

Reward cooperators and punish defectors.

If people obey such a rule, then everyone will have an incentive to cooperate rather than to defect. Different societies can have very different definitions of a "cooperator," depending on the society's ethics and values. However, any ethics and values will only persist if they are enforced. And they will be enforced only if people follow the basic social rule.

The basic social rule can support any type of group. It can bind together a charitable organization or a criminal gang. In particular, the basic social rule is needed in order to bind together the strangers doing tasks for one another in the market.

For example, if you order a product over the Internet and it turns out to be defective, then you can retaliate by writing a negative review. Other shoppers can read your review and reinforce your retaliation by refraining from purchasing from the offending vendor. Those practices give vendors an incentive to deliver products that meet expectations. If no one rewarded cooperators with good reviews or punished defectors with bad reviews, online shopping would be much riskier.

Implementation of the basic social rule can be quite tricky. How do we know that we are buying from a cooperator and not from a defector? Those who study social behavior see many cultural phenomena as emerging to deal with this problem.

- One theory of mass religions is that they helped people with implementation of the basic social rule. People fear that a "big God" will retaliate against them if they defect.[35] Perhaps even more important, as people signal their fear of a big God (by engaging in rituals of worship, for example), they signal to others that they are coop-erators, which means that they can be trusted. In that

[35] See Ara Norenzayan, *Big Gods: How Religion Transformed Cooperation and Conflict* (Princeton, NJ: Princeton University Press, 2013).

way, religiosity serves to build trust in the society. Note, however, that what increases trust within a religious group can constitute a barrier to trust with respect to people outside the group.

- A legal system administered by government is another important institution promoting trust. Those of us who own property are confident that no one is going to use violence or threats to steal our possessions. That confidence is based on our belief that other people will cooperate with the laws against theft, and that belief is in turn based on our faith that the government will retaliate harshly against those who violate those laws.

- Reputation and "brand loyalty" are phenomena that foster cooperation. If people buy only from businesses with good reputations, then firms will seek to acquire good reputations, presumably by engaging in good practices.

The mechanisms for enforcing the basic social rule have important shortcomings. Societies face the problems of deception, abuse of power, and demonization.

We do not have time to carefully study everyone with whom we interact. We use simple heuristics and signals to decide where to place our trust. That leaves us vulnerable to deception.

For many years, wealth manager Bernie Madoff succeeded in deceiving many rich people into believing that he was enabling them to earn consistently high returns on their investments. In fact, he was raising money from some investors to pay off others, in what is known as a Ponzi scheme. Eventually, he ran out of new investors, and the scheme was exposed.

People often send signals of trustworthiness that help them get away with defector behavior. For example, someone may outwardly display obedience to religious rituals but violate that religion's moral codes regarding personal conduct or business ethics.

Salespeople and politicians tend to be more successful if they sound like they are our friends. Some of them become masters of deception.

Abuse of power is another practical problem. We have seen people place faith in government to help implement the basic social rule. An effective government gives people confidence that defectors will be punished and that cooperators will be rewarded. That confidence helps induce more cooperation and less defection.

To implement the basic social rule, government officials are granted unique powers. As anti-government philosopher Michael Huemer puts it, government officials exercise the right to coerce and their citizens are tasked with a duty to obey.[36] But will those unique powers be used for their intended purpose?

Government enforcement of the basic social rule puts the rulers in the position of deciding what constitutes cooperation and what constitutes defection. It is always tempting for a government official to reward mere personal loyalty as if it were social cooperation and to punish dissent as if it were social defection.

The authors of the U.S. Constitution thought long and hard about how to limit the abuse of power by government officials. The authors devised a system of checks and balances. As a result, Americans have been more fortunate than the citizens of many other countries, where abuse of power is rampant. Still, we must be concerned with the abuses of power that do occur. No society has managed to establish institutional arrangements for implementing the basic social rule without government. Yet no form of government always prevents officials from abusing power. In fact, Henrich writes:

> Over time, history suggests that all prosocial insti-
> tutions age and eventually collapse at the hands of

[36] Michael Huemer, *The Problem of Political Authority: An Examination of the Right to Coerce and the Duty to Obey* (New York: Palgrave Macmillan, 2012).

self-interest, unless they are renewed by the dynamics of intergroup competition. That is, although it may take a long time, individuals and coalitions eventually figure out how to beat or manipulate the system to their own ends, and these techniques spread and slowly corrode any prosocial effects.[37]

Government officials are not the only people who can misapply the basic social rule. The heuristics that ordinary people use to identify defectors can be misguided. Sometimes, we condemn as defectors people who are actually decent citizens, a process that might be termed "demonization." For example, the general public may demonize people as defectors on the basis of their ethnicity or their occupation.

In many societies throughout history, anyone who engaged in profit-seeking behavior was viewed with suspicion. In such societies, cooperation meant doing military service or physical labor, with merchants and traders regarded as defectors. Deirdre N. McCloskey argues that a shift in attitudes toward giving dignity to the latter occupations was the key to economic modernization.[38]

[37] Henrich, *Secret of Our Success*, p. 170.

[38] Deirdre N. McCloskey, *Bourgeois Dignity: Why Economics Can't Explain the Modern World* (Chicago: University of Chicago Press, 2010).

Henrich indirectly provides support for McCloskey's thesis. He argues that prestige is a very important factor in cultural learning:

> Across human societies, we see that seeking prestige, often more than wealth itself, drives much human behavior. However, prestige derives from success, skill, or knowledge in locally valued domains. While not infinitely malleable, what constitutes a *valued domain* is amazingly flexible. The differential success of societies and institutions will hinge, in part, on what domains are valued.[39]

For commercial society to develop, commerce must be a valued domain. Today, many people condemn highly paid executives using terms that suggest that those executives are defectors who are taking advantage of the rest of society. Is that an appropriate characterization, or is it demonization?

In short, there are many possible institutional solutions to try to implement the basic social rule, which is required to foster the trust necessary for specialization to be fully realized in a modern economy. Signals and heuristics help us trust other people with whom we interact only occasionally.

[39] Henrich, *Secret of Our Success*, p. 139 (emphasis in original).

Our confidence in government leads us to believe that cooperators will be rewarded and defectors will be punished, and that in turn makes us more willing to cooperate. Our cultural beliefs about what constitutes cooperation help determine whether merchants, traders, and other capitalists are encouraged to contribute to economic development or are demonized and driven away.

At any point in time, it is impossible to state with certainty that the way we label people as cooperators or defectors is correct. It is impossible to know which of the many customs, rituals, and social norms that we have inherited can be discarded as superfluous or harmful, and which of them may be vital for helping implement the basic social rule constructively.

We have seen, however, that each of the mechanisms for implementing the basic social rule has flaws and pitfalls. Signals and heuristics can be faked. Government officials can abuse the authority that is granted them. And cultural prejudices may be wrongly aligned against groups that actually contribute to economic welfare. That is why it is important that we try to focus on the evolution of social institutions. Instead, the MIT approach to economics tends to look for theoretically optimal outcomes while assuming away social and institutional constraints.

7

Finance and Fluctuations

Since 1850, if not before, severe downturns in economic activity have been associated with financial crises. In the United States, we had the Panics of 1873, 1893, and 1907, the Great Depression, and the financial crisis of 2008. Two other major downturns, in 1974–75 and 1980–82, are known as "oil recessions," because in each case a disruption in world petroleum markets played an important role. However, they were also periods in which bank lending fell sharply, particularly for home mortgages.

In a specialized economy, financial intermediaries perform essential functions with respect to time and risk. Financial intermediation allows people to trade across time. It allows people to take advantage of risk pooling, specialization in the analysis of risk, and specialization in monitoring managerial behavior in the context of risk. The functions performed by financial intermediaries enhance trust in the economy. At the same time, financial intermediaries themselves depend on trust.

For specialization to take place, people need to trust that the work that they perform today will yield goods and services that they can consume in the future. We know that a surgeon is better off performing surgery and paying someone else to mow her lawn, rather than mow her lawn herself. However, she cannot directly trade surgery for lawn mowing. Instead, she trades indirectly, through the institution of money.

Money is one form of financial intermediation that enables people to trade across time. In an advanced economy, with its indirect, roundabout forms of production, trading across time is pervasive. For example, suppose that you want to build a fruit business. You will plant trees this year, and in the future, you will harvest and sell the fruit. You need funds today that you will only be able to repay over a period of years.

A consumer who wants to buy a house, or a business that wants to finance an investment in new capacity, needs to obtain funds now in order to undertake a project that will generate value in the future. They are natural borrowers. Other people and businesses have temporarily idle funds that they can lend. They are natural savers.

Financial intermediaries in general, and banks in particular, address a mismatch between the desires of natural savers and borrowers. As savers, we want our funds to be immediately available should we suddenly need them. Also, we want to be assured that when we seek to withdraw our funds, at least our principal will be returned. That is, we want our financial assets to be liquid, with minimal risk.

As borrowers, individuals and firms do not want to have to repay loans suddenly at the whim of the lender. Instead, they want to repay on a gradual schedule, allowing them time to earn the income needed to be able to afford repayment. Also, many borrowers want to engage in risky projects, such as starting a new business or buying a home whose value could fluctuate. As a result, the liabilities that borrowers prefer to issue are illiquid and carry more than minimal risk.

As households, we wish to hold safe, short-term assets and to issue risky, long-term liabilities. Financial intermediaries accommodate that desire by doing the opposite.

Financial intermediation involves layers. For example, consider the fruit orchard. One way to fund a project to plant fruit trees would be to issue shares in the project. If the fruit trees cost $100,000 to plant and the company creates 1,000 shares, then each share will be priced initially at $100.

Over the years, the value of those shares will then rise or fall depending on the health of the trees and on the state of the market for their fruit.

Savers who might purchase shares in the fruit trees will face several challenges. First, they may not know much about fruit growing or the fruit market, which makes it difficult for them to assess the risks and returns of their investment. Second, they may be uncomfortable holding an investment whose value can rise or fall, because they may need funds just at a time when the value of the investment has fallen. Third, they may not be sure whether the managers of the fruit orchard will "loot" the business by taking large salaries or by scrimping on maintenance.

Some of those problems can be addressed by having the business raise a portion of the funds by borrowing. Perhaps the business will issue only $20,000 in shares and will borrow the remaining $80,000 by issuing bonds, promising to repay the principal and a fixed rate of interest over time. Principal and interest on bonds are owed regardless of how well the fruit orchard project pans out. Savers who lend to the firm by purchasing its bonds instead of shares will have a more predictable path of cash flow and less to worry about with regard to management behavior.

The debt contract puts a gun to the head of managers. They must repay the debt on schedule, or they will lose control of the firm. (If the firm defaults on its debt, then its lenders can force it into bankruptcy, in which case the lenders take ownership of the firm's assets away from its shareholders.)

For savers who hold debt of the firm, their position is not perfect. If they suddenly need cash, they will have to find someone to whom they can sell the firm's bonds. Depending on the state of the market when the saver chooses to sell bonds, the saver could take a loss. In addition, holders of the firm's bonds must spend resources monitoring the firm to ensure that its management is adhering to the terms in the debt contract.

As a further step in financial intermediation, a bank can purchase the firm's debt, with the bank offering the public a combination of shares in the bank stock and bank deposits. Bank deposits can be withdrawn at any time. That factor eliminates the risk to a saver of having to suddenly sell bonds and perhaps take a loss.

The bank can also undertake the effort to evaluate the fruit industry and to monitor the specific firm's management to see that it lives up to the terms of the debt contract. As a saver, if I switch from holding the bonds of many firms to holding a bank deposit, my information-gathering problem is reduced from learning about all of the firms in which I hold debt to one of learning about the bank.

A firm that issues both debt and equity is a financial intermediary. A bank is another financial intermediary. Many layers of financial intermediation exist in today's economy, and new forms of intermediation are always being developed.

When a bank gives customers short-term deposits backed by long-term loans, that is known as maturity transformation. In part, the bank is able to do that because it is pooling the funds from many depositors. The bank holds a small cash reserve, but otherwise it has funds tied up in long-term loans. It counts on the statistical likelihood that on any given day, only a fraction of customers will want to withdraw their deposits. The bank's use of pooling means that any one customer can make a complete withdrawal from the bank's small cash reserve, as long as not too many customers seek to withdraw at once. Even though much of the savers' deposits are tied up in long-term loans, the bank can still process the typical pattern of cash withdrawals.

The other transformation that intermediaries undertake is risk transformation. An intermediary takes on risky projects while issuing low-risk liabilities.

To some extent, risk transformation is also based on pooling. If one intermediary backs many projects, then the disappointments will be averaged in with successes.

However, much risk transformation is based on evaluating information. When a bank makes a loan to a business, it carefully evaluates the projects that the business is undertaking in order to ensure that there is a high probability that the loan will be repaid. When the manager of a pension fund invests in shares of stock, the fund manager evaluates the companies to assess their prospects.

When we invest through a financial intermediary, we do not independently evaluate the firms to which the intermediary relays our savings. People who make bank deposits do not evaluate the bank's loan portfolio. People who put money into a managed mutual fund do not evaluate the stocks in the fund's portfolio. If you were to "see through" the intermediary, then you would not need the intermediary to begin with.

What we do attempt to evaluate is the trustworthiness of the intermediary. We make that determination on the basis of reputation. Reputation is typically based on a combination of past performance, advertising, third-party recommendations, and government support.

(One interesting note: it appears that, on average, the reputation of active stock portfolio managers is better than it ought to be. Economists have compared the performance of actively managed funds with those that simply try to match a broadly diversified stock index, and the majority of actively managed funds do worse, at least after we include the cost of their fees.)

In looking at financial intermediaries, economists often ask why individuals cannot undertake the intermediary's tasks themselves. Thinking about that question helps clarify the role of intermediaries, particularly since financial intermediaries do not exist outside the context of the rest of the economy: ultimately, it is individuals who own the shares of financial intermediaries, so that the assets and liabilities of the intermediaries are assets and liabilities of individuals.

For example, in a famous paper, Franco Modigliani and Merton Miller argue that if individuals "see through" the financial structure of the firm to its underlying projects (in our fruit orchard example, that would mean that ordinary individuals know everything about the characteristics of the fruit trees and the fruit market), they will not care how much or how little debt (as opposed to shares of stock) is used to fund those projects. Individuals will choose their exposure to the underlying projects regardless of the firm's financial structure. For example, if the fruit tree firm uses a conservative financial structure, with mostly shares and little debt, but an individual wants to take a large gamble on the fruit trees, the individual can borrow funds to buy the firm's shares on margin. Another individual, who wants very little exposure to the downside risk of the fruit trees, will hold few shares of stock in the fruit tree firm and will instead prefer to hold bonds or other low-risk assets.[40]

In reality, individuals do not see through the financial structure. Most individuals do not wish to delve deeply into the specific prospects of the fruit orchard. Instead, they prefer to hold debt (or better yet, bank deposits) rather than shares. The shareholders (which may be professional investment firms) are willing to put more effort into evaluating the prospects of the fruit orchard.

In fact, in an economy where everyone tries to "see through" banks and other financial intermediaries, the cost of matching savers with investment projects would soar. Complete transparency in banking would require every depositor to study the minuscule details of every loan. Instead, risk transformation undertaken by financial intermediaries is necessarily opaque, with the bank keeping most information to itself and inviting individuals to trust its reputation.

The importance of reputation makes financial intermediaries fragile. They are subject to shifts in sentiment. When people are very trusting of its reputation, an intermediary can expand and fund many risky, long-term projects. For example, in the late

---

[40] Franco Modigliani and Merton Miller, "The Cost of Capital, Corporation Finance and the Theory of Investment," *American Economic Review* 48, no. 3 (1958): 261–97.

1990s, Internet stocks had a reputation for having great prospects, and many new Internet businesses were able to sell shares to the public at high valuations. In many cases, the actual business performance failed to live up to expectations. In the spring of 2000, the "bubble" popped, the prices of Internet-based companies plunged, and for several years, it became difficult for Internet businesses to sell shares to the general public.

The importance of reputation makes government backing highly beneficial to financial intermediaries. One hundred years ago, banks had to exert effort to persuade depositors that their funds were safely invested. Today, in the United States, the Federal Deposit Insurance Corporation (FDIC) takes care of that. The FDIC provides government backing for all but the largest bank deposits. In turn, that means that the FDIC is liable for the risk-taking behavior of banks, and it attempts to regulate such behavior.

A financial intermediary can benefit from the backing of government; the converse is also true. That is, when governments need to borrow money (historically, to finance wars; more recently, to finance chronic peacetime deficits), they rely on banks. The result is that often large banks and government have a cozy relationship, based on mutual dependence.[41]

[41] See Niall Ferguson, *The Cash Nexus: Economics and Politics from the Age of Warfare through the Age of Welfare, 1700–2000* (New York: Basic Books, 2001).

Keynesian economist Hyman Minsky hypothesized that financial intermediation goes through a cycle with three phases.[42] In its most conservative phase (which Minsky called "hedge finance"), firms borrow only when they can repay principal and interest on loans using current profits. In an intermediate phase ("speculative finance"), firms can repay interest using current profits, but they must leave at least some of the principal outstanding. They continue to be in debt, but their debt does not grow. In the wildest phase ("Ponzi finance"), firms must borrow in order to pay interest, and their debts pile higher.

Translating the Minsky cycle into our terms, we would say that during the hedge phase, financial intermediation has a poor reputation, so that savers are skeptical of maturity transformation and risk transformation. Consequently, relatively few risky, long-term projects can be undertaken. During the speculative phase, financial intermediation has a better reputation, savers place more trust in intermediaries, and more risky, long-term projects can be undertaken. During the Ponzi phase, people place unwarranted faith in financial intermediaries, and even wildly risky projects can be funded (think of

[42] Minsky's own writing is notoriously difficult to follow. For a clear exposition of his ideas, I recommend L. Randall Wray, *Why Minsky Matters: An Introduction to the Work of a Maverick Economist* (Princeton, NJ: Princeton University Press, 2015).

the online pet stores and other "dot-com" stocks that took off during the Internet bubble before collapsing).

Minsky's "financial instability" hypothesis is that those phases naturally follow one another. In our terms, when intermediaries behave conservatively, savers lose nothing, and the reputations of intermediaries improve. That result leads intermediaries to behave more aggressively. For a while, they continue to back projects that are mostly sound, so that reputations improve further. When reputations reach a sufficiently high level, at least some intermediaries channel funds to very dubious projects. Eventually, the losses from those projects start to seep through to savers, the intermediaries' reputations collapse, and savers force them to pull back to the most conservative behavior.

In hindsight, the financial crisis of 2008 illustrates how reputations of intermediaries can suddenly shift. Intermediaries held securities backed by home mortgages. Each year, the risk embedded in the mortgage loans increased, but for a while the securities performed well, primarily because rising house prices gave borrowers the wherewithal to avoid having to default. As long as mortgage defaults were rare, trust in intermediaries remained high. However, when house prices began to fall, borrowers began to default in large numbers, and losses started to seep through to holders of the mortgage securities. The reputations of many major financial institutions collapsed. We will return to this episode in the section on policy in practice.

You will find that in standard economics, financial intermediation per se, as described above, plays no role. Instead, most basic macroeconomic textbooks summarize financial markets in relation to interest rates (indeed, "the" interest rate) and the quantity of money. Macroeconomists model the economy as a nonspecialized GDP factory, in which there is only one type of output and one price. I will return to this issue in the section on macroeconomics and misgivings.

From our perspective, it seems plausible that conditions in the financial sector play a role in amplifying fluctuations in economic activity and employment. With specialized, roundabout production, financial intermediation is embedded in every business. If financial intermediaries must shrink because of a sudden loss of reputation, then that could disrupt many patterns of specialization and trade, and it could lengthen the time it takes for new patterns to emerge.

Suppose that a grocer and a bank have a long-term relationship in which the bank finances the grocer's inventory. If that bank has to suddenly curtail its lending, then it may be impossible for the grocer to establish a relationship with a new bank. The grocer may go out of business. Other firms eventually may be able to grow using funds from other banks, but relationships between firms and banks take time to develop.

Another way that financial markets are involved in booms and busts is through speculation. Adair Turner points out that much of the growth in credit in recent decades has been used to finance real estate purchases.[43] To the extent that real estate investment boosts land prices, it does not add any real capital to the economy. However, both people who own land and savers who lend (through financial intermediaries) to homebuyers find that their wealth is increasing, and they may spend more. If there is a subsequent crash, they have to rein in spending. That consequence forces a rearrangement of patterns of specialization and trade, as businesses that have expanded to serve consumers whose wealth increased only temporarily must adjust to a lower volume of business.

That does not mean that all economic fluctuations originate in the financial sector. Instead, it could be that shifts that take place elsewhere are amplified as they hit the financial sector.

Overall, I see economic fluctuations as taking place against a backdrop of major dislocation. That is, my interpretive framework suggests that booms originate with events such

[43] See Adair Turner, *Between Debt and the Devil: Money, Credit, and Fixing Global Finance* (Princeton, NJ: Princeton University Press, 2015).

as major discoveries or innovations, which provide growth and reasons for optimism. The boom is propelled further by increases in financial intermediation, but excesses can emerge. Those excesses produce unsustainable patterns of specialization and trade. When that unsustainability is exposed, painful adjustments are required.[44]

For example, the period from 1920 to 1940, which includes the Great Depression, was one in which small motors changed agriculture and manufacturing, which were the most important sectors of the economy. The internal combustion engine helped power tractors, which allowed farms to grow more crops with fewer workers. It also made possible trucking, which altered economic geography. Trucking enabled more efficient use of land, as food for cities and towns could now be grown much farther away. It also reduced the advantage of cities located on rivers or major rail lines while giving other cities and towns much better transportation and trade opportunities than they had enjoyed previously.

[44] This interpretive framework owes a great deal to Charles P. Kindleberger, who was a professor of economic history at MIT. Kindleberger's approach to economics was more old-fashioned and eclectic than that of the typical MIT professor. He in fact credited the heterodox Minsky with inspiration. See Charles P. Kindleberger and Robert Z. Aliber, *Manias, Panics, and Crashes: A History of Financial Crises*, 6th ed. (New York: Palgrave Macmillan, 2011).

Meanwhile, the small electric motor changed the shape of factories. Previously, factories had been "vertical," covering several stories, so that every machine could draw power from a single gigantic engine on the ground floor. Small electric motors made a "horizontal" factory possible, because each machine could have its own source of power. The spread of the horizontal factory was a major change that took place in this period.

Those trends helped boost productivity, even as economic activity declined during the Great Depression. Indeed, economic historian Alexander Field argues that America's highest productivity growth took place during the 1930s.[45]

Perhaps the disruption to patterns of specialization and trade that took place in the 1930s reflected longer-term developments as overlaid by a speculative boom in the 1920s and a financial contraction in the 1930s. Overall, the economy ended up in 1950 where the longer-term developments took it. But along the way, it followed a rising, falling, rising path as financial intermediation fluctuated.

Similarly, one can argue that the Internet and the emergence of China and India represented the important sources

[45] Alexander Field, *A Great Leap Forward: 1930s Depression and U.S. Economic Growth* (New Haven, CT: Yale University Press, 2012).

of economic dislocation from 1990 through 2015, disrupting many patterns of specialization and trade. Meanwhile, financial expansions took place in the late 1990s and from roughly 2003 through 2007, with a sharp financial contraction in 2008 and 2009. Over the entire 25 years, the economy has been adopting new patterns of specialization and trade. Employment has risen in education and health care, but the number of manufacturing production workers has declined. People with advanced degrees have seen their incomes rise sharply, whereas those without college degrees have tended to fall behind. The positive aspects of this transition seemed most prominent during the financial booms, whereas the adverse aspects became more pronounced during the financial busts, especially the post-2008 period.

8

Policy in Practice

Economic reasoning is essentially discursive reasoning in comparative institutional analysis.
> —Peter Boettke, "Sound Economic
> Reasoning Teaches . . ."

Mainstream economists in the MIT tradition can be very
interventionist with regard to policy. They look at markets as
machines that generate predictable outcomes. Policymakers
can tinker with those machines to improve the outcomes. The
economist's task is to advise the policymaker.

That approach makes two troubling assumptions. One
assumption is that the economist's model is sufficiently powerful to justify overriding market prices. The other assumption is that the political process is sufficiently clean to
implement the policy correctly. Instead, I would argue that, as

Peter Boettke would have it, the economist's task is to explain to the public how one might compare the institutional *processes* of the market and of government.

Those of us who emphasize specialization see markets as trading networks that are constantly undergoing evolution. Rather than look for particular interventions, we raise the question of which institutional mechanisms serve to support the process of specialization and enable it to continue to evolve in a favorable direction.

I think that the best way to illustrate that difference is by using examples. I will look at one example of a specific market, which is the market for housing finance. I believe that one can generalize from this example to see the shortcomings of economic modeling and also the difference between the theory of policy intervention to address market failures and the actual conduct of policy.

The conventional economic approach to policy problems, in the mechanistic MIT tradition, uses far less information than what is available to regulators, which in turn is less information than is processed by the market. The economist builds a simple mathematical model, incorporating little or no institutional detail.

In the context of an economist's simple models, an ideal outcome always exists. Usually, there is predictable deviation from the ideal outcome, on the basis of the assumptions built into the model. Those predictable deviations from ideal are termed a "market failure," and the model is used to recommend specific policies to correct such a failure. However, the extent to which the policy setting in practice deviates from that in those simple models is rather alarming.

Consider housing finance. Understanding housing finance in the United States requires much institutional and historical background. To avoid a long interruption of the main body of this work, I put that background information in the appendix. There, I go into a lot of detail, for a good reason. I believe that it is the general practice of economists to ignore such detail, with the result that their models are badly disconnected from reality. I hope that most readers will take the time to go through the appendix.

In the years that led up to the 2008 financial crisis triggered by mortgage defaults, the government intervened to encourage more leniency on the part of lenders and to tilt in favor of mortgage loans originated to be sold rather than to be held by the originator. What market failures would justify such interventions?

In theory, a market failure is a circumstance in which the incentives of individuals work against the general interest.

Because of the misalignment of incentives, there is either underprovision or overproduction of some good or service. For example, if the production of steel causes air pollution, then in the absence of government intervention, more steel is likely to be produced than would be optimal. On the other hand, if security guards benefit neighbors regardless of whether they personally contribute to pay for the guards, then in the absence of government intervention, or at least some form of collective action in the neighborhood, there will be underprovision of security guards.

In the years leading up to the financial crisis of 2008, did too much home building or too little home building take place? In some locations, there may have been too little building, but in the areas where the crisis hit, it would appear in hindsight that there was too much home building. However, at the time, hardly anyone recognized that factor as a market failure, and no policymakers called for a reduction in home building or homeownership.

In the years leading up to the financial crisis, did too much mortgage lending or too little mortgage lending take place? Once again, in hindsight, it seems pretty clear that homebuyers and homeowners were taking on too much debt. However, at the time, policymakers were more inclined to argue that the market failure was that lenders were too strict than to argue that the market failure was that lenders had become too lenient.

In the years leading up to the financial crisis, did too much lending take place through mortgage-backed securities or through "originate-to-hold"?[46] In hindsight, the securities proved to be the greater problem for the financial system. However, at the time, regulators were happy to see mortgages held in the form of securities, and in the appendix, I explain how they tilted bank capital regulations in favor of this approach and against originate-to-hold.

In short, we find that in the real world—in contrast to the world of simple economic models—it can be difficult to ascertain whether the market is providing too much or too little of a particular good or service. In the case of housing and housing finance, it would seem that if there were market failures, government policy in practice served to exacerbate such failures rather than to mitigate them.

The problems of housing policy in practice go beyond this single episode. The most common justification for government intervention in housing finance is that it promotes

[46] Originate-to-hold is the traditional approach in which the bank that originates the mortgage also provides the funds and receives the payments. In the "originate-to-distribute" approach, those roles are divided up, and mortgage debt is packaged into tradable securities. See the appendix.

homeownership. However, this justification is weak in many respects, including the following:

- It is unclear whether homeownership is a public good. Although I may benefit from owning my home, that benefit does not count as a public good. Only if someone else benefits from my owning my own home do we say that homeownership is a public good. In fact, society could be at least as well off if there were more renters.[47]

- Even if homeownership is a public good, what mortgage subsidies encourage is indebtedness. I say that it encourages home-borrowership. A better policy would be to subsidize households to save for large down payments to obtain homes.[48]

If more homeownership is the goal, then public policy should aim to reduce the cost of buying a home. Instead, some policies do the opposite. Many cities impose restrictions and regulations on new construction, driving up the price of housing.

[47] See Arnold Kling, "Who Needs Home Ownership?" *The American*, October 30, 2012, https://www.aei.org/publication/who-needs-home-ownership/.

[48] See, for example, Joseph Gyourko, "A New Direction for Housing Policy," *National Affairs* 23 (Spring 2015), http://www.nationalaffairs.com/publications /detail/a-new-direction-for-housing-policy.

The United States maintains an antiquated, fragmented, and expensive system for transferring property titles. People who buy homes are forced to purchase "title insurance," which would be completely unnecessary under a different legal system.[49]

In general, American housing policy in practice can be summarized as if it followed two principles: (a) subsidize demand, particularly for mortgage credit; and (b) restrict supply. The combination of subsidized demand and restricted supply has one clear consequence: prices for houses are higher than they would be otherwise. Whether the amount of homeownership is higher or lower than it would be with less government intervention is ambiguous.

The policy pattern that consists of subsidized demand and restricted supply is not limited to the housing market. It pervades government regulation of industry. For example, in education, the government subsidizes demand by helping pay for education, and it restricts supply by limiting accreditation. In health care, government subsidizes demand through Medicare, Medicaid, and various tax breaks and subsidies for obtaining health insurance. Yet it restricts supply by regulating the practice of medicine, requiring a "certificate of need"

---

[49] For those interested, look up the term "Torrens title."

before a new hospital may be built, and requiring inventors to undertake extensive studies to demonstrate the efficacy of their treatments to the satisfaction of the Food and Drug Administration.

From the standpoint of the theory of market failure, the subsidized-demand, restricted-supply pattern almost never makes sense. If a market failure results in underproduction of a good, then it makes sense to subsidize both demand and supply. If a market failure results in overproduction, then it makes sense to restrain both demand and supply. Subsidies for demand and restrictions on supply inherently work at cross-purposes.

However, from the standpoint of another theory, called public choice, in which government policy tends to serve concentrated interests rather than to address market failures, it is understandable for government to subsidize demand and restrict supply. In a specialized economy, we know that the market for what you produce affects your well-being much more than the market in any one of the myriad goods and services you consume. Thus, concentrated interests develop on the supply side, not on the demand side. The pattern of subsidized demand and restricted supply is what you would expect to result from interest-group politics in a specialized economy.

In the case of housing, there are strong, concentrated interest groups of current homeowners, who want to see restrictions on supply. The acronym for their political outlook is NIMBY—not in my back yard. There are other strong, concentrated interest groups that encourage home purchasing financed by mortgage credit: the National Association of Realtors®, the National Association of Home Builders, and the Mortgage Bankers Association. Each has members in every congressional district, and they collectively form perhaps the most powerful lobby in Washington. Thus, we should not be surprised to find that the demand for mortgage financing and home purchases is subsidized, even as housing supply is restricted in many jurisdictions.

Clifford Winston, an economist who surveyed the gap between market-failure theory and government practice, writes,

> The bulk of microeconomic theory has devoted far more attention to identifying and characterizing potential sources of market failure than to recognizing and analyzing the causes of government failure.[50]

[50] Clifford Winston, *Government Failure and Market Failure* (Washington, D.C.: Brookings Institution, 2006), p. 104.

Winston's concerns are shared by other observers of government in practice.[51] Moreover, because supplier interests are persistent, bad government policies are difficult to change. For example, widespread agreement exists among environmentalists and economists that biofuel subsidies cause environmentally damaging expansion of cropland and drive up fuel prices, but those subsidies are politically difficult to eliminate because they benefit corn growers.

In the case of housing finance, the influence of supplier interests on policy has been deep and pervasive. Wall Street firms have leaned very hard on regulators and elected officials to support the market for mortgage-backed securities.[52]

One can argue that it is not the economist's job to fix the political system. Instead, an economist should prepare to offer advice as if the political actors are concerned with the general interest.

However, I believe that economists owe concerned citizens a warning that flaws in the market process are not easily corrected by shifting power to the political process. I believe

[51] For example, see Peter H. Schuck, *Why Government Fails So Often: And How It Can Do Better* (Princeton, NJ: Princeton University Press, 2014).

[52] See Michael Lewis, *Liar's Poker: Rising through the Wreckage on Wall Street* (New York: W. W. Norton, 1989); and Bethany McLean and Joe Nocera, *All the Devils Are Here: The Hidden History of the Financial Crisis* (New York: Portfolio/ Penguin, 2010).

that the main lessons that one should remember from the example of housing policy are the following:

- In hindsight, better outcomes could have been achieved with different regulatory policies. However, that does not mean that regulators suffered from a weakness of regulatory philosophy. Instead, as you will see in the appendix, given the high degree of specialization in mortgage finance, regulators were not in a position to understand every element in the process and to anticipate every possible point of weakness. One of the key points of failure—the process for assigning risk ratings to mortgage-backed securities—was not on any regulator's radar screen.

- In hindsight, regulatory initiatives undertaken before the financial crisis of 2008, on balance, probably served to promote practices that turned out to be unwise. Regulatory policies tended to steer lenders toward making more high-risk loans rather than toward maintaining rigorous standards for approving mortgage borrowers. Regulatory policies tended to encourage banks to delegate risk measurement to the securities-rating agencies rather than to rely on traditional ways of assessing mortgage risk using the originate-to-hold model.

- Concentrated interests have played an important role in setting housing policy. A significant disconnect exists between the theoretical idea of public goods and the determination of public policy in practice.

The orthodox approach asks: "What is the optimal outcome? What policy intervention can produce that outcome?" This approach assumes away all government failure. It assumes away the ability of private-sector actors to adapt to solve problems or to circumvent regulatory intent.

Instead, the alternative approach is to ask, "Which institution is likely to arrive at the best solutions for problems of this type?" That is a more subtle and difficult question.

The alternative approach does not always militate against centralized solutions. For example, water sanitation in a large urban area is likely to be better handled by a central authority than through negotiations among individual homes and businesses. Simply too many interdependencies exist to make it feasible for a decentralized market to solve the urban sanitation problem.

Similarly, air quality would be more easily managed with a central authority. Basic transportation infrastructure, including the placement of roads and traffic signals, is also likely to be better designed if a central authority undertakes the task than if it is left to individual decisions.

Sanitation and basic infrastructure are examples of goods where the benefits are widespread and roughly equal among citizens, and where a lot of interdependence exists among decisions. Centralization is less appropriate when many citizens do not benefit from the good, or when citizens differ radically in the way that they value the good, or where individual transactions can be undertaken with relatively little effect on parties not involved in those transactions.

9

Macroeconomics and Misgivings

Next, let me turn from the relatively narrow topic of housing finance as an example of microeconomic policy to the broader issue of macroeconomic fluctuations. What can policymakers do to maintain high levels of employment and low levels of inflation?

My interest in macroeconomics was sparked by my first course in macro, taught by Frank Pierson of Swarthmore College when I was a freshman. Macroeconomics continued to fascinate me through my undergraduate years, in part because they coincided with two dramatic events of the early 1970s: (a) President Nixon's imposition of floating exchange rates along with wage and price controls in 1971 and (b) the

Arab oil embargo of 1973, which was followed by increased inflation and a severe recession.

After graduation, I joined the newly created Congressional Budget Office as a research assistant in the Fiscal Analysis Division, which focused on macroeconomic analysis. We worked with the large computer models of the economy that were popular at that time. However, we noticed that the models performed so poorly at prediction that the computer forecasts were always altered manually by the human proprietors of the models. Moreover, when I went to graduate school at MIT in 1976, I soon learned that the large statistical macroeconomic models were in disrepute in the academic community.

Economists have to weigh two broad criteria in assessing their interpretive frameworks. One criterion is *internal*. We look for consistency with economically rational behavior. We have norms of what constitutes rational choice by individuals, and we tend to trust the predictions of models that treat people as making decisions according to those norms more than predictions that assume that people persistently violate them.

The second criterion is *external*. We look for consistency with observable data. In the case of macroeconomics, we would prefer a model with useful explanations and predictions of the behavior of unemployment, inflation, and other important macroeconomic statistics.

In the mid-1970s, academic macroeconomics became focused almost exclusively on the *internal* criterion. The statistical models were not working very well, anyway. Meanwhile, the academic macroeconomists developed an intense fascination with solving the mathematical problem of figuring out how a representative household would form expectations of future variables that were "rational" in the sense that they extracted all available signals about the future.

Expectations took on great importance in the context of a widely held theory that recessions were caused by errors made by businesses and households in their forecasts of the aggregate price level. I always found that theory of recessions highly implausible, and so I considered the focus on "rational expectations" to be misguided. At the time, one could not have a career in macroeconomics without being a "rational expectations" modeler, so mainstream macroeconomics and I parted ways. I believed then and continue to believe that more important causes of unemployment exist than this sort of expectational error.

The mainstream view implied that as long as the central bank helped make the aggregate price level predictable, no recessions would occur. Coincidentally, from the mid-1980s until the financial crisis of 2008, the economy had only two recessions, both mild. That period came to be known as the Great Moderation.

After graduate school, I took a job as an economist at the Federal Reserve Board. There, the more I looked at macroeconomic statistics, the more doubtful I became about the ability to use those data to test macroeconomic theories. In the end, we have just one economy. We cannot run controlled experiments. We can only observe the pattern of history, and many plausible theories exist to explain this historical pattern. That limitation makes macroeconomics a frustrating field for anyone who hopes to settle arguments about theory in a scientific manner.

I gradually lost interest in macroeconomics altogether, and I turned instead to finance. In 1986, I left the Fed to work for a different government agency, the Federal Home Loan Mortgage Corporation. Known as Freddie Mac, it was spun out as a private firm a few years after I joined. My focus there was on modeling interest-rate risk and credit risk in housing finance.

In 1994, I left Freddie Mac to launch one of the first commercial sites on the World Wide Web. I then spent six years with this project, called homefair.com, which benefited from the Internet frenzy of the late 1990s when we were bought out by another site, called homestore.com, shortly after its company had its initial public offering. That foray into entrepreneurship took me even further from macroeconomics.

It was the financial crisis of 2008 that revived my interest in macro. The financial crisis and its aftermath were quite unforeseen by macroeconomists. Even *ex post*, the theory that recessions are caused by mistaken forecasts of the aggregate price level seemed to be a poor candidate for an explanation of the long, deep recession that took place. That realization finally forced macroeconomists to turn away from their internal obsessions with rational expectations and instead to pay attention to the real world. It revived my interest in macroeconomics, in part because housing finance, which I had learned about at Freddie Mac, was so heavily implicated in the crisis.

Many macroeconomists soon recognized that the theoretical work focused on "rational expectations" was not helpful in explaining the events of 2008. Widespread dissatisfaction exists with the lines of macroeconomic research that were pursued between the mid-1970s and 2008. Nearly all macroeconomists believe that significant changes to mainstream macroeconomics are now necessary.

My own view is that what is wrong with macroeconomics is the use of a "representative agent" to stand for all of the decisions that affect an economy. The conventional approach ignores specialization and instead treats the entire economy as one business, which I call the GDP factory. Most macroeconomists remain reluctant to abandon the GDP-factory approach, even as they try to open up their thinking to allow a greater role for finance and market psychology in their framework.

Since I consider specialization one of the most important characteristics of a modern economy, I am inclined to discard the conventional approach. Before I spell out my criticisms of the conventional approach, let me sketch out my own views.

In my preferred framework, all of the sources of unemployment are adjustment problems. In a specialized economy, at any point in time, some people may find themselves employed in ways that are not profitable. Such jobs are not sustainable, and the workers will be let go.

Sometimes, the dislocation is only temporary. For example, if an automobile manufacturer's dealers report having too many unsold cars on their lots, then the manufacturer may shut down production for a month or two before recalling workers to start making cars again.

More often, however, job cuts are permanent. Some firms go out of business. Meanwhile, firms that remain in business will constantly adjust up and down the size of various departments as they try to remain as profitable as possible.

The adjustment problem that the economy faces is to reemploy workers who have lost their jobs, especially those whose job losses are permanent. In fact, that adjustment problem is very complex and generally is handled very well. The government data known as the Job Openings and Labor Turnover Survey shows that each month about 4 million workers are let go, and about the same number are hired. The difference between the two, which is the net gain or loss in employment, is typically less than 5 percent of that 4 million. When the net loss amounts to 200,000 or more for several months in a row, we describe the job market as very weak.

In economic jargon, adjustment problems can be categorized into static problems and dynamic problems. A static problem exists in taking the job structure as given. The dynamic problem is the need for entrepreneurs to discover new jobs.

Static adjustment problems, which have been explored by conventional macroeconomists, can in turn be divided into two main types. One type of problem is mispricing. The wage desired by would-be workers can exceed the wage at which they can be profitably employed. The other main problem is mismatching. Jobs exist for workers at wages for which they are willing to work, but the workers have not found those matches.[53]

[53] There is also work by Peter A. Diamond, Dale T. Mortensen, and Christopher A. Pissarides that in a way combines the mispricing and mismatching problems. They shared the Nobel Prize in Economics in 2010. See the nobelprize.org webpage for 2010, http://www.nobelprize.org/nobel_prizes/economic-sciences/laureates/2010/.

In my view, the dynamic adjustment problem is more significant. At any given time, the jobs that might employ idle workers do not exist. The new jobs have to be discovered by businesses, through a trial-and-error process. Existing firms launch new projects. Entrepreneurs create new firms. Those that succeed will create sustainable jobs. Enterprises that fail, however, will not be able to help the unemployed.

The static adjustment problems can be described using the mathematical techniques of the economic engineers, who believe that they can control the economy. However, the process of dynamic adjustment, with its evolutionary characteristics, is more difficult to model and to control.

Dynamic adjustment is how we get out of an economic mess. But how do we get into economic messes in the first place?

In my view, no two recessions are exactly alike. Each unhappy economy is unhappy in its own way, in part because individuals and businesses learn from the past and instead make mistakes that are slightly different from the ones that were made before. However, some phenomena do tend to appear in many recessions, include post-mania crashes in asset prices, abrupt reductions in credit availability, sharp changes in some key prices (such as the price of oil or the price of real estate), and important underlying trends in the structure of jobs.

Charles Kindleberger, building on the ideas of Hyman Minsky, has offered a framework for looking at manias and crashes. Kindleberger adds a concept he calls "displacement," in which a major event causes prospects for wealth to increase in a country. Examples include winning a war, incorporating an important new technology, or taking advantage of important new trading opportunities. Such events can give rise to manias.

In the United States, for example, a decade after victory in World War I, we experienced the mania of the Roaring Twenties. Decades later, the collapse of the Soviet Union and the rise of computers were followed by an Internet mania and then a housing mania.

Manias can create unsustainable patterns of specialization and trade and postpone the adjustment to structural change. Manias involve very optimistic valuations of real estate, stock market shares, tulip bulbs, or other assets, leading people to believe that they are wealthier than they truly are. Patterns of specialization and trade that are established to cater to people with illusory wealth will be revealed as unsustainable once asset prices return to normal (or, more often, below normal).

Meanwhile, difficult long-term adjustments may be impeded or disguised. The mania of the 1920s helped temporarily disguise the impact of the adjustment to the tractor, the truck, and the electric motor. Many jobs involving manual labor in factories and farms were becoming unsustainable. The new jobs ultimately were in wholesale and retail trade, but those jobs typically required a high school education. An important part of the adjustment process was that by 1950, a generation of poorly educated workers had aged out of the labor force. Meanwhile, the United States experienced the Great Depression of the 1930s.

Similarly, the housing mania of the early 2000s helped temporarily disguise the impact of the adjustment to the changes brought about by the Internet and globalization. Once again, the composition of the workforce appears to be undergoing a shift, as signified by a low rate of labor force participation.

That focus on dynamic adjustment and longer-term structural problems makes economic policy more challenging than it has appeared since John Maynard Keynes published *The General Theory of Employment, Interest, and Money* in 1936. Keynes argued that deficit spending by the government can be a solution to the problem of unemployment. Economists in the Keynesian tradition also usually argue that expansion of the money supply can be a solution to the problem of unemployment. But from the perspective that unemployment represents a dynamic adjustment problem, there is little reason to believe that Keynesian fiscal or monetary stimulus provides any solution.

Keynesian economics is steeped in ambiguity. A large scholarly literature is devoted to the topic of "What Keynes really meant." Theoretical issues have been debated ad nauseum by economists for at least the past 80 years.[54]

In fact, I often think that ambiguity has benefited Keynesianism. One version, which I call popular Keynesianism, is taught to undergraduates and appeals to journalists, politicians, and the intuition of noneconomists. The other version, which is taught in graduate school and which I call rigor-seeking Keynesianism, claims to achieve mathematical sophistication and internal consistency that is lacking in popular Keynesianism.

Popular Keynesianism is embedded in first-year economics textbooks. Students are shown the "circular flow" of spending: households obtain goods and services from businesses, and businesses obtain labor and capital from households. In the opposite direction are money flows: businesses pay households for labor and capital, and households pay businesses for goods and services.

[54] For my take on the history of macroeconomic thought, you can read Arnold Kling, "Memoirs of a Would-Be Macroeconomist," 2013, http://arnoldkling.com /essays/papers/macromemoir.pdf.

The circular flow presents an economy with no price mechanism. Completely divorced from the standard economics of supply and demand, the circular flow makes it appear that quantities depend only on other quantities.

Examining the circular flow, the student sees that the money that households have to spend comes from payments by businesses, and those payments in turn come from household spending on goods and services. It is easy to imagine a recession as something that interrupts or slows down that circular flow.

Factors that increase or decrease the circular flow can be termed "injections" and "leakages" (Frank Pierson was using those terms back in 1971 when I took my first economics course). Business investment provides an injection into the circular flow. Household saving provides a leakage from the circular flow (even though it is by saving that households supply capital to businesses). When we add fiscal policy to this framework, government purchases become injections, and taxes become leakages. Thus, an increase in spending or a cut in taxes will increase the circular flow, leading to more output and employment.

The central bank also plays a role in popular Keynesianism. In textbooks, when the monetary authority reduces interest rates, it leads households and businesses to inject more spending into the circular flow. Economic journalists will even describe the central bank as giving households more money to spend, although that is incorrect, confusing monetary policy with fiscal policy.

Popular Keynesianism offers the noneconomist a satisfying narrative to explain economic fluctuations. Every household understands that if the demand for its labor were to increase, it would have more money to spend. Every businessperson understands that if the demand for the firm's output were to increase, it would have more reason to hire additional workers. If an economy is in a recession, it then seems quite natural to think of it as a business suffering from insufficient demand and as a household suffering from underemployment.

However, the set of all businesses and households is not the same as a single business or household. To someone well trained in the laws of supply and demand, popular Keynesianism is not intuitive at all. In fact, it violates a number of standard microeconomic precepts:

- In conventional economics, we teach that the fundamental economic problem is scarcity. People have unlimited wants and scarce resources. In popular Keynesianism, the notion of deficient aggregate demand describes an economy in which some resources are superfluous, and that is because wants are limited.

- In conventional economics, saving promotes capital formation. Businesses deploy savings to acquire capital goods. The interest rate balances the rate of intertemporal substitution in production (how much businesses can increase output tomorrow by undertaking investment today) with the rate of intertemporal substitution in consumption (the consumer's preference to satisfy wants now rather than later). In popular Keynesianism, rather than financing investment, saving takes spending out of the circular flow and leads to unemployment. The interest rate does not play a balancing role. Saving and investment are treated as separate decisions.

- In conventional economics, price adjustment serves to eliminate surpluses and shortages. In popular Keynesianism, a surplus of goods exists without any mitigating downward adjustment of prices. For example, the shortfall in aggregate demand leads to a surplus of labor, without any mitigating downward adjustment of wages.

Rigor-seeking Keynesianism addresses the problems with popular Keynesianism. Rigor-seeking Keynesians allow for prices to operate, but they incorporate short-term impediments to price adjustment. They replace the Keynesian separation of saving and investment with a mathematical model of "intertemporal optimization" by consumers, meaning that consumers choose to shift consumption between the present and the future, depending on current conditions and expectations of future conditions.

The rigor-seeking Keynesian approach is prevalent in graduate school and in academic journals, where it is sometimes referred to as New Keynesianism. However, it has little or no influence as an interpretive framework for policymakers or for the general public. For example, in an interview with Martin Wolf, Lawrence Summers said,

> I would have to say that the vast edifice in both its new Keynesian variety and its new classical variety of attempting to place micro foundations under macroeconomics was not something that informed the policymaking process in any important way.[55]

Summers was reflecting on his tenure as head of the National Economic Council at the start of the Obama administration.

The two forms of Keynesianism help support each other. Popular Keynesianism is useful for trying to convince the

[55] Lawrence Summers, "A Conversation on New Economic Thinking," interview with Martin Wolf of the *Financial Times* at the Bretton Woods Conference, April 8, 2011, http://larrysummers.com/commentary/speeches/brenton-woods-speech/.

public that macroeconomists understand macroeconomic fluctuations and how to control them. Rigor-seeking Keynesianism is used to beat back objections raised by economists who are concerned with the ways in which Keynesianism deviates from standard economics, even though the internal obsessions of rigor-seeking Keynesianism have no traction with those making economic policy.

However, both versions of Keynesianism have ignored specialization and instead think in relation to the GDP factory. Accordingly, my verdict is that neither version of Keynesianism is on the right track.

Most mainstream economists believe that the nation's central bank plays a crucial role. In the United States, many economists, and educated people in general, regard the Federal Reserve Board as a sacred institution. Founded during the Progressive Era, the Fed is an independent agency stocked with experts, primarily economists. Its task is to achieve macroeconomic objectives by regulating banks, manipulating interest rates, and controlling the supply of money.

The Fed has many critics among conservatives. They argue that the Fed's leaders are too enamored of the use of discretionary powers. Those critics maintain that the Fed tends to overreact to economic conditions, keeping its foot on the economy's metaphorical gas pedal for too long and then slamming on the brakes, causing overly sharp recessions. Or to use a metaphor generally attributed to Milton Friedman, the Fed is like a fool in the shower, alternately making the water far too hot or far too cold.[56]

My views on this topic are unorthodox. I believe that both supporters and critics attribute to the Fed more power than it actually wields. In short, this is what I believe:

> *Money and prices are social conventions. The Fed should be thought of as just another big bank. It does not control what people accept as money, and it does not control the habitual behavior that causes the movement of aggregate price indexes.*

Before elaborating on this belief, let me sketch out the more orthodox view. Macroeconomics can be thought of as beginning with the formula

$$M \times V = NGDP,$$

[56] I have not found the citation of when Friedman used this metaphor. However, James Tobin once wrote, "An amateur shower-taker suffers cycles of scalding and freezing water." (Tobin himself argued *in favor* of Fed discretion and *against* the view that the Fed is as clumsy as an amateur shower-taker.) See James Tobin, "Discussion," in *Controlling Monetary Aggregates III*, Federal Reserve Bank of Boston Conference Series no. 23, 1980, p. 73.

where M stands for the quantity of money, V stands for the "velocity" of money, and $NGDP$ stands for nominal gross domestic product, meaning the total amount of market-traded goods produced each year, valued at then-current prices.

If I tell you that NGDP increased by 10 percent last year, that does not tell you that 10 percent more goods were produced. To know how much more was produced, you have to know how much of the 10 percent increase came from changes in prices, that is, from inflation. Let us write down another formula:

$$NGDP = P \times Y,$$

where P is an index of prices, and Y is real GDP, intended to measure the true volume of production. Putting those two formulas together, we have

$$M \times V = P \times Y,$$

which is the standard textbook formula.

If we assume that V is constant, then we have crude monetarism. NGDP (or $P \times Y$) is pumped up or down by changes in the quantity of money. In crude monetarism, the details of patterns of specialization and trade, and of financial intermediation in particular, are entirely irrelevant. All that matters is the quantity of money.

Suppose that our economy is a factory that produces plastic water bottles that sell for $10 each. The amount of money in circulation is $2 billion, and the velocity of money is 5, meaning that money changes hands 5 times each year. $M \times V$ will be $10 billion, which means that $10 billion in water bottles will be sold. Dividing by the price of $10, we can predict that 1 billion water bottles will be sold in this economy.

Instead of assuming that V is constant, Keynesians introduce more variables into macroeconomics by saying that the velocity of money depends on the interest rate. That leads to a system of equations that relates spending, the quantity of money, and the interest rate. However, this macroeconomic tradition, which derives from an interpretation of Keynes given by John Hicks,[57] still has no role for specialization and trade or for financial intermediation.

On paper, the formula appears flawless. In practice, I do not think it tells us anything. Official statistics exist only for M, P, and Y. There is no direct measure of velocity. V is simply what you get by solving for it using the formula, in other words by dividing $(P \times Y)$ by M.

[57] J. R. Hicks, "Mr. Keynes and the 'Classics'; A Suggested Interpretation," *Econometrica* 5, no. 2 (1937): 147–59.

Even the measures of P, Y, and M are problematic. For government statisticians, estimating NGDP is conceptually straightforward. You have to measure all of the market transactions in *final* goods and services. The statisticians must be careful not to double-count the $5 that the store paid to the manufacturer for the water bottle and the $10 that you paid to buy the water bottle from the store.

But separating NGDP into P and Y is more difficult. If NGDP went up by 10 percent last year and prices went up by 5 percent, you may want to infer that P and Y both went up by 5 percent. However, you do not know the extent to which the quality of goods improved. If the quality went up by 5 percent, then we should treat the price change as zero and treat all of the increase in NGDP as a real increase in output. Statisticians are forced to make estimates of quality change, but they have no absolutely reliable way of doing so. Over periods of one year or less, quality change may not be very significant. However, over periods of five years or more, quality change can matter a great deal. Indeed, some goods will be entirely new, and some goods that were important in prior years will have very little value today.

Defining the money supply, M, is even harder. The intuition for using the formula $MV = PY$ is that people need money to engage in transactions. If the only way people pay for goods and services is to use currency, then the amount of currency in the hands of the public is a sensible measure of M, and V is a measure of how rapidly currency circulates through the economy.

However, it has been a long time since people relied on currency for most of their transactions. When I studied economics, paper checks were a popular medium for transactions, and economists tried to accommodate that by defining money as currency in circulation plus the amount on deposit in checking accounts. In the 21st century, I see people paying with plastic, meaning credit cards and debit cards. Moreover, other payment media are also gaining in popularity, particularly for Internet transactions.

What happens if our measure of M has little correlation with the way that people pay for things? In that case, changes in our measure of M will be independent of changes in NGDP. If M goes up and NGDP does not change, then our calculation of V will go down proportionately. Our formula will tell us that changes in M are always offset by proportionate changes in V in the opposite direction.

On the other hand, one could try to find measures of M that allow for modern transaction mechanisms and are correlated with NGDP. The problem with such measures is that they do not yield a definition of M that is under the control of the central bank.

The central bank can control the quantity of money only if we define money very narrowly. However, if we want to define money in a way that correlates to NGDP, we must define money very broadly. The apparently airtight monetarist formula is actually limp with slack, because the two definitions of money do not coincide.

Thus, I say that money is a social convention. That is, what people use in ordinary transactions changes with technology and custom. Instead, treating the quantity of money as if it were analogous to a physical phenomenon like mass or length is a futile and misleading exercise.

Some monetarists argue that the point that people use different media for transactions is irrelevant. The Fed can still transact in financial markets and treat future NGDP as its "target." That is, if projected NGDP is lower than desired, the Fed can buy securities, and conversely if projected NGDP is higher than desired, the Fed can sell securities.[58]

In fact, any financial institution can choose to buy or sell securities using its forecast for NGDP as its basis. However,

---

[58] See Scott Sumner, "The Case for Nominal GDP Targeting," Mercatus Center, George Mason University, Arlington, VA, 2013, http://mercatus.org/publication /case-nominal-gdp-targeting.

no one would describe Citigroup or Goldman Sachs as targeting NGDP. Too many other financial intermediaries exist for any one of them to be able to control the economy.

To me, it seems right to think of the Fed as just one of many large financial intermediaries. Like other intermediaries, its liabilities are less risky and of shorter duration than its assets. When the Fed purchases more assets, it is expanding its role as a financial intermediary. However, there are too many other financial intermediaries for the Fed to be able, by itself, to control the economy.[59]

One of Hyman Minsky's aphorisms is,

> Anyone can create money. The problem lies in getting it accepted.[60]

Any individual or organization can create a debt instrument, or an IOU. If many people are willing to buy and sell that IOU, then it acts as money. The willingness of people to buy and sell different IOUs has changed in response to technology

[59] Few other economists share my perspective that the Fed is but a small player in large financial markets. They include Deirdre N. McCloskey, "Other Things Equal, Alan Greenspan Doesn't Influence Interest Rates," *Eastern Economic Journal* 26, no. 1 (2000): 99–101; and Fischer Black, *Exploring General Equilibrium* (Cambridge, MA: MIT Press, 1995).

[60] Wray, *Why Minsky Matters*, p. 94.

and shifts in cultural norms. That is why I say that money is a social convention.

The view that money is a social convention is tied to a view that prices are a social convention. That view is troublesome to those who seek, and claim to find, a mechanical explanation for the overall behavior of prices.

The orthodox view of money offers a straightforward explanation for inflation. Prices rise rapidly when the central bank prints too much money. That makes the orthodox view seem useful for explaining periods of high inflation, such as the European hyperinflations of the 1920s or the high inflation in the United States in the 1970s.

In the 1920s, some countries, including Germany, experienced hyperinflation. Prices rose at phenomenal rates, approaching 100 percent per month. Money creation was very rapid, and money lost value with equal rapidity. More recently, Zimbabwe experienced a similar trauma.

However, central banks by themselves do not go on wild sprees of monetary expansion. The fundamental source of hyperinflation is unsustainable government budget deficits. When a government cannot obtain sufficient funding through taxes and long-term borrowing, it must resort to printing money to pay for salaries, purchases of goods and services, and benefits to constituents. The recipients of government payments do not want this rapidly depreciating paper, but they have no choice other than to accept it and then try to spend it as quickly as they can. Until the government undertakes reforms to bring spending back down in line with tax collections, its ever-increasing printing of money does indeed drive down the value of the paper that it uses as payment.

Within the interpretive framework that I prefer, hyperinflation is a fiscal phenomenon. As Fischer Black put it:

> The government must passively supply whatever money the private sector demands. It cannot "print money" without running massive deficits. I find no scope for monetary policy. In other words, money doesn't matter.[61]

Normally, there is no hyperinflation, because ordinarily government spending does not exceed the country's capacity to obtain revenue from taxation and from long-term borrowing. In normal times, most prices remain stable, with some prices rising and some prices falling. Changes in relative prices (prices of computers falling, college tuition rising) are much more dramatic than changes in the overall rate of inflation.

---

[61] Black, *Exploring General Equilibrium*, p. 78.

Concerning inflation, Fischer Black wrote:

> The inflation rate is indeterminate. . . . It can be whatever people think it will be. (The money supply will passively accommodate whatever the inflation rate turns out to be.) . . .
>
> If people expect a certain inflation rate, that's what they get, because they set prices and wages to match their expectations.[62]

People get used to basing calculations on what they think of as normal inflation. Usually, their idea of normal comes from recent experience. Therefore, inflation tends to have a lot of inertia. That characteristic is good, because otherwise the information and prices would be very noisy, and markets would function poorly as a result.

Over the past 70 years, inflation in the United States has typically stayed in the range of 1 percent to 5 percent. However, inflation broke out of that range significantly in the 1970s, reaching highs of close to 15 percent. In the early 1980s, inflation began to ebb, receding to its normal range by the end of the decade.

[62] Ibid., p. 80.

The orthodox framework interprets the 1970s' inflation as an acceleration caused by excessive monetary growth. In the orthodox view, the Great Inflation ended in the 1980s with a change in Federal Reserve policy that reduced the rate of money creation.

From the standpoint of my alternative framework, the 1970s' inflation is more of an anomaly. One possible explanation is that the habitual behavior of people changed. They began to expect high inflation, and they incorporated such expectations into labor contracts and other long-term arrangements.

One factor that may have shifted expectations regarding inflation was the breakdown of international currency arrangements. From the end of World War II until 1971, the United States pegged the dollar to gold, and other countries pegged their currencies to the dollar. There was some flexibility in those arrangements, but they may have contributed to expectations of fairly stable prices. However, as the United States ran large budget deficits, in part because of the Vietnam War in the 1960s, gold drained out of the United States, and in 1971, President Nixon was forced to abandon the gold peg and switch to a regime of floating exchange rates. Although he introduced wage and price controls at the same time, the inflationary effect of abandoning the gold peg may have ultimately overcome that crude attempt to control prices by fiat.

Another, possibly-related factor that shifted inflation expectations in the 1970s was the rise in price of oil. Starting in 1973, the oil-producing countries achieved some success in restricting supply. As oil prices rose, people began to accustom themselves to seeing frequent price increases in all goods and services, creating a sort of self-fulfilling cycle. Those expectations gradually receded when the price of oil collapsed in the early 1980s.

Inflation is one of two key macroeconomic variables. The other is unemployment.

Keynes published *The General Theory* during the Great Depression, when the main problem in the United States and Europe was not inflation, but unemployment. To this day, in explaining fluctuations in employment, all Keynesian and monetarist frameworks are based on the concept of "aggregate demand." This concept treats the economy as a GDP factory. When demand is high, the GDP factory runs at full capacity. When demand is low, part of the factory shuts down.

If there really were just one form of output, say, bananas, I am certain that there would be no unemployment. If an unemployed worker were to appear, an entrepreneur would offer to employ that worker at a slightly below-market wage and produce bananas that could be sold at a slightly below-market price at a profit. Alternatively, the entrepreneur could hire the worker with no cash wage involved and instead pay the worker in bananas.

In fact, any economic model with just one or two goods is likely to be misleading, even downright silly.[63] In reality, many types of goods exist, and many types of tasks are involved in producing goods. A job does not consist of producing a fraction of generic output. Instead, a job consists of a small subset of the millions of tasks that are undertaken in a modern economy.

The tasks that make up a job are not random. The set of tasks that make up a job must add sufficient value to cover the cost of undertaking those tasks.

The value added of a set of tasks is highly dependent on context. In 1900, a typical horseshoe maker added more value than a typical software developer. Today, the opposite would be true.

---

[63] For example, see Paul Krugman, "Baby-Sitting the Economy," *Slate*, August 14, 1998, http://www.slate.com/articles/business/the_dismal_science /1998/08/babysitting_the_economy.html. Krugman attaches significance to the example of a babysitting cooperative, where the members pay one another in the form of chits for future services. Members who wish to accumulate chits for later use will offer babysitting services. With too many members doing so, there will be excess supply. Note that in this example, the economy has no investment. Because there is no investment, savings has nowhere to go. Not surprisingly, a desire to save causes problems in this context. In the real world, there are uses for savings, and for me that makes the story of the babysitting co-op rather unconvincing.

Thus, we arrive at the following definition of a job:

A job is a context for performing a particular small set of tasks that can be exchanged for the means to obtain goods and services produced by a far larger set of tasks.

A modern economy consists of many jobs, which reflect highly developed forms of specialization and trade. The patterns of specialization and trade are very complex, and yet no single person is in charge of creating them. The patterns are created by entrepreneurs acting in a decentralized fashion, coordinated by the price system and by the profit incentive.

Because of specialization, employment fluctuates in a modern economy. You become unemployed because the work in which you have specialized can no longer be profitably exchanged. It does not solve the problem for the firm to keep you on the job and pay you in output, because what you produce has nothing to do with what you consume. ("Mr. Jones, I can no longer afford your salary, but if you stay on I'll let you keep a copy of the report you were going to write for me on ways to improve our budgeting process.")

When a business experiences a decline in revenue, that decline reflects conditions specific to the industry and to that firm. Conditions at individual firms and within industries vary more than overall economic performance. Even during booms, some industries suffer from obsolescence, and some firms are unable to remain profitable. Even during recessions, some firms thrive because they are in growing industries, making improvements to production processes, or attracting consumers to innovative products and services.

In an economy with roundabout production, specialization and trade create interdependence among firms. A firm that is involved in the early stages of a production will be affected by conditions in the market for final output. A firm selling final output will be affected by firms involved in the early stages of production.[64] As noted earlier, financial intermediaries are embedded in nearly every business, so that interdependence involving financial intermediation probably plays an important role in fluctuations in economic activity.

Even when unemployment is relatively high, most patterns of specialization and trade will still be sustainable. Unfavorable conditions are limited to particular locations, industries, and firms. Given that problems are likely to be highly concentrated, there is no simple, generic solution.

---

[64] For some empirical confirmation of these patterns of propagation, see Daron Acemoglu, Ufuk Akcigit, and William Kerr, "Networks and the Macroeconomy: An Empirical Exploration," draft for NBER Annual Conference on Macroeconomics, National Bureau of Economic Research, Cambridge, MA, April 14, 2015. Note that their interpretation of these patterns is in line with conventional macroeconomics rather than the ideas expressed here.

A far-off change in government spending, taxes, or monetary policy does little or nothing to address the specific situation of a firm that is no longer efficiently meeting consumer needs or of workers whose skills are no longer highly valued in the market. In fact, two economists who undertook a survey of businesses found that the large fiscal stimulus enacted in 2009 did not cause many firms to hire unemployed workers.[65]

The economy undergoes constant change. Entrepreneurs are constantly undertaking experiments in the form of new businesses. When their experiments succeed, they create new sustainable patterns of specialization and trade. Often as a consequence, other patterns of specialization and trade become unsustainable. The more that firms and workers have dedicated themselves to now-obsolete patterns, the more time and effort are required to find new, sustainable patterns of specialization and trade in which the workers can take part.

Newly unemployed workers may not know how best to respond to layoffs. Perhaps conditions at their firm will revive, and they will be recalled. Perhaps other firms in their industry are eager to take advantage of their skills. Perhaps they need

[65] Garett Jones and Daniel M. Rothschild, "Did Stimulus Dollars Hire the Unemployed?" Working paper, Mercatus Center, George Mason University, Arlington, VA, August 30, 2011, http://mercatus.org/publication/did-stimulus -dollars-hire-unemployed.

to relocate to a different region. Perhaps they need to change industries. Perhaps they need to acquire new skills.

Meanwhile, entrepreneurs are undertaking experiments. They are trying to start new businesses. Eventually, some of those businesses will take off, and as they grow they will need to dip into the labor pool. However, that process only gradually serves to alleviate unemployment. Because specialization is extensive and production processes are very roundabout, it is not easy to anticipate which new enterprises will succeed in establishing new patterns of specialization and trade that are sustainable. As the process unfolds gradually, unemployment can remain high.

Firms and workers are constantly undertaking the required adjustments. Data on labor turnover in the United States show that 4 million to 5 million jobs are created and destroyed each month. However, the net change in total employment rarely shows an increase or decrease of more than 300,000 jobs. Thus, if 4 million workers are hired but 4.3 million workers are fired, that change means a decline in employment that earns front-page news.

It is fair to ask why gains and losses in employment are not even more balanced than they are. How can existing patterns of specialization and trade become unsustainable before new patterns are established? Why do we observe net reductions in employment over a period of several months that cumulate into the millions? I do not believe that we have completely satisfying answers to those questions.

If you think of the economy as a GDP factory, then unemployment will be cured by having workers return to the jobs from which they were laid off. Indeed, temporary layoffs have sometimes taken place in some industries, notably construction, automobiles, and steel, where workers were rehired after excess inventories had been reduced. Those industries employed a significant share of workers in the three decades following World War II, and some of the postwar recessions can properly be called inventory recessions.

Since the 1980s, such temporary layoffs due to inventory fluctuations have become a smaller proportion of job losses, and permanent job losses have been a larger component of increased unemployment. One reason for the decline in inventory fluctuations is that the share of the economy devoted to goods production has fallen. Other sectors, notably health care, education, and finance, have become increasingly important. The other factor is that inventory cycles have been dampened as firms deployed information technology effectively.

As we saw in the section on finance and fluctuations, some factors can amplify periods of job loss. Patterns of specialization and trade can depend too much on consumers whose spending is based on transitory increases in wealth caused by speculative euphoria. That appears to be a major factor in the recession that accompanied the drop in house prices in 2007–10.

Because the wealth that was created by the housing bubble was illusory, some of the patterns of specialization and trade that were established before the crash turned out to be unsustainable. The subsequent job losses are not temporary, and the bubble-driven patterns of trade cannot be restored. Permanent job losses can be cured only by discovering new patterns of sustainable specialization and trade. If government intervention is going to speed the recovery from recessions, such intervention is going to have to contribute to that discovery process.

Consider some of the specifics of the stimulus package that was enacted in 2009, the American Recovery and Reinvestment Act. It is hard to see how some of the most important components of the package would create new sustainable patterns of specialization and trade.

For example, there was the "cash for clunkers" program. That program gave rebates to buyers of new cars between late July and late August of 2009. The program shifted some auto purchases forward in time, but that in itself does not create new patterns of sustainable specialization and trade.[66]

[66] See Atif Mian and Amir Sufi, "The Effects of Fiscal Stimulus: Evidence from the 2009 Cash for Clunkers Program," *Quarterly Journal of Economics* 127, no. 3 (2012): 1107–42.

Another program involved subsidies for companies involved with "green energy." Such subsidies are not evidently a way to create patterns of sustainable specialization and trade. Patterns that are sustainable do not require subsidies. Patterns that are not sustainable cannot survive once subsidies are ended. Indeed, several prominent recipients of subsidies went bankrupt not long after receiving government funds.

If there are visionaries who can see that certain innovations in energy will prove sustainable, then they are not precluded from risking their own funds and persuading others to risk funds on such investments. For the "green energy" program to add to the patterns of sustainable specialization and trade in the economy, the government would have to employ visionaries with superior understanding of energy technology and economics rather than those who rely on private-sector funding.

Other programs included temporary reductions in taxes and temporary increases in means-tested benefits. Although those approaches might have altered some spending patterns for a few months, it is difficult to see how they would have resulted in new patterns of sustainable specialization and trade.

What can the government do to speed the process of discovering new patterns of specialization and trade? I am afraid that is a rather difficult challenge. Although the Keynesian "gas pedal" has never worked the way its advocates have claimed, I do not have a simple, powerful alternative.

One of the most interesting periods for the creation of new patterns of sustainable specialization and trade was the decade following World War II. From a standard Keynesian perspective, the sharp drop in government spending and the release of millions of previously conscripted soldiers into the labor market might have resulted in a deep depression. Instead, the private sector recovered and created sufficient jobs to restore full employment.

The war itself put new combinations of people together to solve problems. That had an effect on subsequent business formation. For example, David Halberstam profiled William Levitt, the entrepreneur of Levittown housing developments. Halberstam describes how Levitt honed his thinking while serving in the U.S. Navy during World War II:

> At night, Levitt sat around with other young men in the Seabees, all of whom had backgrounds in building and contracting, and they would brainstorm about their work—what they were doing that day, how to do it faster, and also what they would do after the war. The Navy, Bill Levitt said years later, provided him with a magnificent laboratory with which to experiment with

low-cost mass housing and analyze it with his peers—
a chance he might never have had in civilian life.[67]

Military service pulled people out of their hometowns. Army
buddies who otherwise would not have met ended up starting
businesses together.

Dan Senor and Saul Singer, who examined Israel's entrepreneurial culture, also note that many business partner-
ships are formed by men who met doing military service.
More than that networking, however, the authors emphasize
the technical training and cultural norms inculcated by the
Israeli army.[68]

In the United States, attending college often helps young
people build social networks. Those in turn lead to business
relationships.

Many institutions attempt to catalyze interactions among
people. Conferences serve to bring people together. Since
the early days of the Internet, people have tried to use online
forums to forge connections.

Still, there may be opportunities for interpersonal connection that the private sector is missing. For example, I believe

[67] David Halberstam, *The Fifties* (New York: Villard Books, 1993), p. 133.

[68] Dan Senor and Saul Singer, *Startup Nation: The Story of Israel's Economic
Miracle* (New York: Twelve Books, 2009).

that urban and rural America have become increasingly separate. It also appears that urban areas themselves have become increasingly segregated by class.[69] It could be that government policies that encourage people to spend time with others of different backgrounds would generate ideas for new businesses. Of course, one is entitled to be skeptical about government's ability to carry out such an initiative in a way that is not heavy-handed or counterproductive.

Overall, the U.S. economy seems to have experienced a drop in dynamism over the past 30 years. Researchers have found declines in the rates of new business formation[70] and in household mobility.[71]

---

[69] See Charles Murray, *Coming Apart: The State of White America, 1960–2010* (New York: Crown Forum, 2012). See also Robert D. Putnam, *Our Kids: The American Dream in Crisis* (New York: Simon and Schuster, 2015).

[70] Ian Hathaway and Robert E. Litan, "Declining Business Dynamism in the United States: A Look at States and Metros," Brookings Institution, Washington, D.C., May 5, 2014, http://www.brookings.edu/research/papers/2014/05/declining-business-dynamism-litan; Ryan Decker, John Haltiwanger, Ron S. Jarmin, and Javier Miranda, "The Secular Decline in Business Dynamism in the U.S.," 2013, http://econweb.umd.edu/~haltiwan/dhjm_jep_5_17_2013.pdf.

[71] Raven Molloy, Christopher L. Smith, and Abigail Wozniak, "Declining Migration within the US: The Role of the Labor Market," working paper, Federal Reserve Board, Washington, D.C., 2015, http://www.federalreserve.gov/pubs/feds/2013/201327/201327pap.pdf.

Some of that decline may be due to changes in the structure of the economy. One factor is that the largest secular growth has been in health care and education, where it is very difficult to compete against established institutions. Another factor is that the age distribution of the population has shifted upward, which might lead to less flexibility and less risk taking. Another factor is the rapid decline in the value of physical labor relative to work that requires cognitive skills.

In the contemporary economy, skills may be more specific to particular jobs, making it difficult to substitute one worker for another. That aspect may encourage more longer-term relationships between firms and workers. However, by the same token, a worker who loses a job will take longer to find a new one.

To the extent that government policies impede hiring, starting a business, and moving to a new location, it would make sense to try to change those policies. Many economists see harm in restrictions on high-skilled immigration, because there is a high rate of new business formation among immigrants. They see harm in occupational licensing rules, which inhibit competition and hamper mobility (because occupational licenses are often not transferable across state lines). They see land-use regulations in major cities holding back their economic potential and also hampering mobility.[72]

The main point here is that better economic outcomes arise when patterns of sustainable specialization and trade are formed. Those patterns do not come about as a result of tinkering undertaken by the Federal Reserve or by deficit spending undertaken by Congress. It requires the creative, decentralized, trial-and-error efforts of thousands of entrepreneurs and millions of individuals seeking the best way to use their talents. Probably the best thing that the government can do to encourage new forms of specialization is to rethink existing policies that restrict competition, discourage innovation, and retard mobility.

[72] See Brink Lindsey, "Low-Hanging Fruit Guarded by Dragons: Reforming Regressive Regulation to Boost U.S. Economic Growth," Cato Institute white paper, June 22, 2015, http://www.cato.org/publications/white-paper/low -hanging-fruit-guarded-dragons-reforming-regressive-regulation-boost-us.

10

Concluding Contemplation

I hope that this book stimulated you to think about specialization and trade as powerful and important features of modern society. Above all, the extreme specialization that exists today creates a very complex economic system.

Mainstream economics in the Samuelson tradition tries to boil down market processes to a few equations. It claims to identify government solutions to market failures and to fluctuations in economic activity. One goal of this book has been to suggest that such attempts fall to pieces when confronted with the complexity of the real economy.

Another goal has been to suggest unsolved problems to think about. One problem is how society can sustain the trust that is needed for specialization and trade, given that each of the mechanisms that help promote trust has drawbacks. Another problem is how to deal with the seemingly inherent instability of financial intermediation. Finally, there is the problem of how to maintain a better balance between the creative and destructive forces of the economy, so that we do not experience long periods of high unemployment as we await the creation of new patterns of sustainable specialization and trade.

Appendix: How Housing and Mortgage Policy Worked in Practice

Let's start with a brief glossary of terms:

Thirty-year fixed-rate mortgage. This type of mortgage is the most common loan used to finance home purchases in the United States. The loan is repaid in equal monthly installments, 12 each year for 30 years, for a total of 360 payments. The monthly payment also includes funds to cover property taxes and insurance, so that the lender knows that those obligations will be met.

Early in the life of the mortgage, most of the monthly payment covers interest, and the outstanding principal declines slowly. As time goes on, more and more of the monthly payment is devoted to principal, and the outstanding loan balance shrinks until the final installment eliminates the debt entirely.

The 30-year fixed-rate mortgage includes two valuable options for the borrower. One option is to prepay the entire outstanding balance of the loan. That option becomes useful if market interest rates fall. For example, if you borrow at 6 percent and mortgage rates subsequently fall to 5 percent, you can reduce your interest cost by taking out a new loan at 5 percent (from the same lender or from a competing lender) and using the proceeds to pay off the 6 percent loan.

The other option allows the borrower to default on the loan while sacrificing only the property secured by the loan. Once the lender completes the foreclosure process and takes possession of the home, in most American states the borrower has no more obligation to repay the loan. (In contrast, in Canada, mortgage loans come with "recourse," meaning that if the lender cannot recover the principal on the loan by selling the foreclosed house, the borrower continues to owe the lender the funds to make up the difference.) Because in most American states the borrower's obligation to repay the loan goes away with foreclosure, if the market price of the house should fall below the outstanding balance on the mortgage loan, the borrower might be financially better off defaulting than by trying to keep up the mortgage payments.

Loan origination. Loan origination is the first step in the lending process. From the originator's point of view, that means advertising and marketing to attract loan applicants, working with the applicant to select specific loan terms, obtaining information from the applicant, and deciding whether to accept or reject the final loan application. The originator disburses the proceeds of the loan to the borrower in order for the borrower to pay for the house. The legal step of purchasing the house is called settlement.

Loan servicing. After settlement, the loan servicer takes over administering the mortgage loan. Servicing the loan means collecting the borrower's monthly payments and applying them to various accounts (property taxes, insurance, principal, and interest). If the borrower falls behind on payments, the servicer is the first to know. The servicer is the entity responsible for sending reminders to the borrower and, if necessary, initiating foreclosure proceedings.

Mortgage-backed security. A mortgage-backed security is a financial asset in some ways similar to a corporate bond. It is created by pooling dozens of similar mortgage loans. The monthly principal and interest paid by the borrowers are passed through to the owners of the security, called the investors.

The mortgage securities market was created by the U.S. government.[73] The first mortgage-backed securities were issued in 1968 by the Government National Mortgage Association Ginnie Mae, with mortgage loans consisting of those made by the Federal Housing Administration (FHA), which guaranteed the payment of principal on each mortgage, even if the borrower were to default. That is, if an FHA borrower defaults, the investor receives the outstanding principal from the FHA. The FHA takes the loss, attempting to recover as much as it can by foreclosing on the property and selling the house.

In 1970, the Federal Home Loan Mortgage Corporation (Freddie Mac) was created as a government agency for the purpose of issuing mortgage securities backed by loans originated without FHA guarantees. It became Freddie Mac's responsibility to pay investors when mortgage borrowers defaulted. Soon, the Federal National Mortgage Association (Fannie Mae) was also issuing mortgage-backed securities.[74]

[73] There had been sporadic attempts to create private mortgage-backed securities, but those had failed to gain a foothold.

[74] Fannie Mae was created in the 1930s. Originally, it was a government agency that purchased loans, primarily those guaranteed by the FHA, using funds raised by issuing debt to investors in government securities. In 1968, the government sold Fannie Mae to private investors, and in the late 1980s, Freddie Mac, too, was privatized. However, the relationship of those entities to the U.S. government remained ambiguous.

Investors had reason to believe that the government would bail out Freddie and Fannie rather than allow those large housing finance agencies to default on their obligations.

Private-label mortgage-backed securities. Private-label mortgage-backed securities are mortgage-backed securities issued, typically by major Wall Street firms, without any government backing. Before the year 2000, very few such securities were issued. Issuance increased rapidly between 2000 and 2006. The firms that pooled the mortgage loans came up with a security structure in which the risk of mortgage defaults was concentrated in one part of the security, enabling the underwriters to market the remaining tranches of the security as low risk. Bond rating firms, such as Moody's and Standard & Poor's, assigned their highest credit ratings, AAA and AA, to those low-risk tranches. This approach was further endorsed by government regulators, who in 2001 ruled that private-label mortgage-backed securities with AAA ratings were entitled to substantial relief from capital requirements.[75]

Subprime mortgages. Unfortunately, there is no generally accepted definition of a subprime mortgage. In the 1970s and

[75] For more on the capital treatment of mortgage-backed securities, and the role it played in the run-up to the financial crisis, see Jeffrey Friedman and Wladimir Kraus, *Engineering the Financial Crisis: Systemic Risk and the Failure of Regulation* (Philadelphia: University of Pennsylvania Press, 2011).

1980s, Freddie Mac and Fannie Mae issued a set of credit standards for mortgages. Their standards defined what were known as "conventional" mortgages. One way to think of subprime mortgages is that they are loans that fall short of meeting the conventional standard. Note, however, that some loans were ineligible for sale to Freddie Mac and Fannie Mae because of their sheer size ("jumbo loans"), for reasons having nothing to do with credit. Note also that Freddie Mac and Fannie Mae were constantly adjusting and adapting their credit standards, which makes it impossible to fix the definition of subprime by referring to their standards.

Credit standards fall generally into three categories, known as the "three Cs": collateral, credit, and capacity.

Mortgage loans are backed by the property, which constitutes the collateral. The ability of the collateral to reduce the lender's risk depends on several factors.

One major factor is the loan-to-value (LTV) ratio. Both common sense and statistical evidence show that loan default propensity rises as the LTV ratio increases. On a $100,000 house, if the borrower makes a down payment of $30,000 and borrows the remaining $70,000, then the LTV ratio of the mortgage is $70,000/$100,000, or 70 percent. That LTV ratio is relatively low, and it gives the lender a lot of protection. If the market value of the house falls to $80,000 and the borrower meanwhile suffers the loss of a job and is unable to keep up the monthly payments, the borrower can sell the house, pay the mortgage, and still keep some of the proceeds from the sale. In contrast, if the buyer of the $100,000 home makes a down payment of just $3,000 and has to borrow the remaining $97,000, then the LTV ratio is 97 percent, which is high. Now, in the scenario in which the price falls to $80,000, the borrower has no incentive to keep up the payments, apart from the value of maintaining a good reputation. By defaulting and letting the lender take possession of the house, the borrower can wipe out $17,000 in excess debt, which is the difference between the $97,000 loan amount and the $80,000 market value of the house.

For many years, Freddie and Fannie set the standard for the LTV ratio at a maximum of 80 percent, or 90 percent if the borrower obtained private mortgage insurance. (Companies specializing in private mortgage insurance earn a fee in exchange for absorbing some of the loss in the case of a mortgage default.)

In addition to the LTV ratio, other factors also influence collateral protection. Compared with investors who buy property for income, owner-occupants tend to strain harder to make payments. Thus, collateral is more protective when the borrower is an owner-occupant.

The value of property is always uncertain, but the value obtained from a market transaction and confirmed by an appraisal is more reliable than the value that is estimated from an appraisal alone. Accordingly, collateral for a cash-out refi—meaning a refinancing of a borrower's mortgage in which the loan amount for the new loan is higher than that of the loan being replaced—is more suspect than collateral for a loan made to purchase a home.

After collateral, the second C is credit. A borrower's credit history is a powerful indicator of the borrower's self-discipline and skill at managing debt. Borrowers with a track record of late payments on credit cards, or who have outstanding balances on their credit cards that are near the maximum permitted by the issuers of the cards, are more likely to get into trouble with their mortgages than are borrowers with less troubling credit histories. Since the mid-1990s, the mortgage industry has used credit scores, which are numerical ratings created by specialized firms employing sophisticated statistical analysis, to assess the credit C.

The third C is capacity. Does the borrower have enough income to be able to afford the monthly payment on the mortgage loan and also pay for other necessities? Does the borrower have enough assets in reserve to enable the loan payments to continue for a few months should the borrower encounter adversity, such as in health or employment?

Capacity can be very difficult to assess. Income is easy enough to measure when someone earns a salary from a large organization. However, many occupations, such as business owner or self-employed professional, do not provide a regular paycheck. In those instances, the loan originator has to evaluate a highly variable income history.

It is in evaluating capacity, the third C, that loan originators traditionally ask borrowers to supply documentation. For example, pay stubs could be used to verify income and employment. Bank statements could be used to verify assets. Supplying such documentation can be difficult for loan applicants who have not been in the same location for a long time and for those who work in occupations that do not come with regular pay stubs.

As they competed for loan applications during the U.S. housing boom of 2000–2006, loan originators increasingly offered "low-doc" and "no-doc" loans. That meant that borrowers were not asked to supply documentation to support the claims made on their loan applications regarding income, employment, and assets.

In principle, one can classify a loan as prime or subprime by comparing it against standards for the three Cs. Does the loan-to-value ratio exceed 80 percent (90 percent with mortgage insurance)? Does the credit score fall below some minimum threshold? Does the borrower show enough income and assets to handle the debts that the borrower will have in place once the mortgage loan is made? And are the borrower's income, assets, and employment status properly documented? If the answer to any of those questions is no, it might be argued that the loan is subprime.

Many of us who have worked in mortgage risk analysis would argue that collateral is the most important C. We would put credit next. The importance of capacity and of documentation of capacity is unclear. That is, the correlation between capacity and loan performance is not as strong as one might expect, but that could be because capacity is often measured inaccurately (which is a legitimate reason to downplay it in mortgage risk analysis). Meanwhile, lack of documentation is a higher risk factor than one might expect. The reason might be because low-doc borrowers overstate their capacity to carry loans (perhaps with the assistance of unscrupulous loan originators), or it might mean that low-doc lending selects riskier borrowers. People who seek low-doc loans may have incomes that are unstable, or they may just lack the discipline to undertake the effort to assemble the required information, and that lack of discipline also affects their ability to manage their finances.

This glossary of terms can help us understand specialization in the context of mortgage lending. In fact, the trend has been for specialization to increase. Fifty years ago, when you borrowed money to buy a house, one bank (or savings and loan association) processed your loan application, provided the funds, and processed your payments. That is, a single firm played all three major roles: loan originator, investor, and loan servicer. Today, that arrangement is known as the "originate-to-hold" model of mortgage lending. In contrast, the more specialized approach is known as the "originate-to-distribute" model, because the loan originator, instead of keeping the mortgage loans that it originates, "distributes" them to investors, who obtain them in the form of securities.

The evolution of mortgage lending has introduced many important new specialists:

- Credit repositories, which keep track of individuals' credit use of all kinds, are the suppliers of the individual credit report that is the basis for assessing the second C of credit.

- Credit-scoring firms specialize in statistical analysis of the data that can be found at the credit repositories.

- Mortgage brokers specialize in taking applications.

- Mortgage bankers use mortgage brokers as sources for business. The mortgage bankers prefund mortgage loans by selling them before settlement to Freddie or Fannie or to a private-label securitizer. (Because loans can fall through before settlement, that forward-selling process is quite tricky to manage.)

- Insurance companies, pension funds, and money management firms specialize in investing in mortgage-backed securities.

- Wall Street firms facilitate trading in mortgage-backed securities. They also played a critical role in structuring private-label mortgage-backed securities into high-risk and low-risk tranches.

- As we have seen, the lending process also has a role for mortgage insurers, loan servicers, the FHA, Ginnie Mae, Freddie Mac, Fannie Mae, and firms that rate the riskiness of securities (like Moody's and Standard & Poor's).

- The specialists that we have discussed so far are involved in dealing with the potential for mortgage loans to default. Mortgage lending also carries with it interest-rate risk, meaning that the value of an investment in mortgage loans or mortgage-backed securities can rise or fall as interest rates fluctuate. Another set of specialists is devoted to the problem of interest-rate risk, which is particularly tricky in the case of mortgage instruments because of the prepayment option.

This degree of specialization poses a challenge for regulators. Regulators cannot be expected to understand every process as well as the specialists themselves understand it. That incomplete understanding makes it almost impossible for regulators to correctly anticipate problems.

Which specialists should have received the focus of regulators before the crisis that hit the housing finance market in 2007 and 2008? The answers are much clearer in hindsight than they could have been at the time.

Housing finance experts, and secretaries of the treasury under both President Bill Clinton and his successor President George W. Bush, voiced concern about the concentration of risk at Freddie Mac and Fannie Mae. However, most of that concern was focused on interest-rate risk. Critics argued that Freddie Mac and Fannie Mae were retaining too many mortgage securities in their portfolios, rather than selling those securities to other specialists in interest-rate risk management. Yet when the crisis came, interest-rate risk played no part.

Before the crisis, some public-interest groups and policymakers had concerns about the credit repositories and about the reliability of credit scoring of individuals. However, there was little or no concern about the process of grading the risk of securities by the major credit-rating agencies. In hindsight, credit scoring was not implicated in the financial crisis, whereas there is a consensus that flaws in the rating of securities were central to the misestimation of risk on the part of financial industry executives and of regulators.

Before the crisis, policymakers criticized lenders for not doing enough to serve borrowers with low incomes or who belonged to disadvantaged minorities. Those criticisms encouraged a general trend toward reducing lending standards. Indeed, there are those who see Washington as the main culprit in undermining the quality of mortgage lending. The Community Reinvestment Act and the affordable housing goals promulgated to Freddie Mac and Fannie Mae by its regulator were arguably a factor.[76]

The lowering of lending standards received no pushback from regulators. Even Edward Gramlich, a member of the Board of Governors of the Federal Reserve who was known

---

[76] This argument is made most forcefully in Peter J. Wallison, *Hidden in Plain Sight: What Really Caused the World's Worst Financial Crisis and Why It Could Happen Again* (New York: Encounter Books, 2015).

as one of the few critics of subprime mortgage lending before the crisis, said in a speech in 2004:

> Despite the caveats, the net social evaluation of these trends is probably a strong positive. The 9 million new homeowners, more than half of whom are minorities and many of whom have lower incomes, suggest that credit and ownership markets are democratizing. Millions of lower-income and minority households now have a chance to own homes and to build wealth; and the vast majority of these new homeowners do not appear to be having credit problems. The rates of serious delinquencies and near-serious delinquencies do raise important warning flags and should inspire renewed efforts to prevent foreclosures, but they do not seem high enough to challenge the overall positive assessment.[77]

In hindsight, I believe that the main problem with mortgage originations in this period is that the LTV ratios soared to 95 percent and higher on many loans. That factor necessarily

[77] Edward M. Gramlich, "Subprime Mortgage Lending: Benefits, Costs, and Challenges," remarks at the Financial Services Roundtable Annual Housing Policy Meeting, Chicago, May 21, 2004, http://www.federalreserve.gov/Boarddocs /Speeches/2004/20040521/default.htm.

created a speculative market, because home equity became a function of price appreciation, rather than the buyer's contribution of a down payment. As lending expanded and house prices rose, even bad loans were repaid (sometimes by the borrower taking out a new loan using the increased house value as collateral). However, when the housing appreciation leveled off, the risky loans were exposed, and a vicious downward cycle ensued.

By 2006, high-LTV lending pervaded the mortgage market. Both nontraditional lenders and traditional lenders subject to regulatory influence were deeply engaged in the practice. Even Freddie Mac and Fannie Mae discarded their formerly strict LTV limits.

Still, I believe it is the case that nontraditional lenders were particularly implicated in originating the riskiest loans. And it seems clear in hindsight that regulators did not understand the way that defaults on those mortgages could cascade through the financial system. The process of mortgage securitization, with its many specialized roles, was simply too complex for regulators to fully grasp.

One of the main tools used by the regulators was risk-based capital regulations for banks. Banks have many types of liabilities, including checking and savings deposits. They also raise funds by issuing shares of stock. Funds raised in that manner are termed the bank's capital. Because deposits and other liabilities are less expensive than stock, banks tend to prefer to have a low ratio of capital to assets.

Regulators set minimum capital requirements for banks. However, to discourage banks from meeting those requirements by spurning low-risk assets in favor of riskier loans, regulators assign risk weightings to different assets. An asset, such as a government-issued bond or a Fannie Mae security, will be deemed low risk by regulators, therefore requiring less capital. Consequently, banks are encouraged to hold such assets.

Starting in the late 1980s, regulatory capital requirements consistently favored mortgage securities issued by Freddie Mac and Fannie Mae over mortgage loans originated by the bank itself. That is, capital requirements tilted the mortgage-lending market to favor the "originate-to-distribute" model over the "originate-to-hold" model. That bias in favor of securitization became even stronger in 2001, when regulators put private-label AAA-rated and AA-rated mortgage-backed securities under the low-risk umbrella.

In hindsight, those risk-based capital regulations were a serious miscalculation. The originate-to-distribute model enabled nontraditional lenders, with no stake in the quality of the mortgages they originated and sold, to thrive. Thus, the quality of the mortgages originated was reduced. Then, the risk was compounded by the poor methods used by the securities-rating agencies, which ended up assigning AAA and AA ratings to tranches that had a much higher risk of default than comparably rated corporate bonds. Even highly rated corporate bonds were not given favorable treatment by regulators, which meant that the assets that banks were encouraged to hold were riskier than the assets that they were discouraged from holding.

Is "originate to distribute" better than "originate to hold" as a means for financing home purchases? I do not believe any expert knows the answer. The originate-to-distribute model incorporates more specialization, which might make it more efficient.

On the other hand, the originate-to-distribute system involves a conflict of interest between originators and investors. Suppose two brothers, Angelo and Roger, are trained to make loan decisions. Roger works for an old-fashioned bank, which holds the loans that it originates. Angelo works as a broker in the originate-to-distribute system.

Roger will be paid by the bank to uphold its credit standards, and if he approves bad loans, he will eventually be disciplined or fired. Angelo, on the other hand, earns a commission only on loans that he can sell to investors. If he fails to uphold credit standards but still manages to sell a bad loan, he earns more money. If he upholds credit standards and turns down a bad loan, he gets nothing. Compared with Roger, Angelo has a bigger incentive to approve bad loans, which is what creates the conflict of interest in the originate-to-distribute system.

The conflict of interest between brokers and investors is not fatal to the originate-to-distribute model. It can be managed by adopting and enforcing contractual relationships among the various parties. Still, it is unclear whether the cost of administering such measures outweighs the benefits of increased specialization. In any case, it is difficult, if not impossible, to point to a market failure that would justify having the government support the originate-to-distribute model by establishing enterprises like Freddie Mac and Fannie Mae and by offering banks favorable capital treatment for holding mortgages in the form of securities.

To anticipate the specific way in which risk-based capital requirements failed, regulators would have needed more specialized knowledge. They would have had to better understand the business model and operating practices of the nontraditional lenders. They would also have had to better understand the complex mathematics, statistics, and modeling assumptions used in structuring mortgage securities and rating the various tranches. Above all, the regulators did not consider the possibility that home prices could experience significant declines, and they were unable to foresee how such declines would cascade through the mortgage finance system.

In general, however, the failure of risk-based capital requirements is something that we can predict. It is always the case that government policymakers are going to lack important information that can be discovered only by participants in the market. Just like a would-be socialist central planner, a regulator faces an insurmountable calculation problem.[78]

[78] I previously made this argument in Arnold Kling, "The Regulator's Calculation Problem," Library of Economics and Liberty, April 6, 2015, http://www.econlib.org/library/Columns/y2015/Klingregulators.html.

Index

Following a page number, an *n* indicates a note.

Libertarianism.org

Liberty. It's a simple idea and the linchpin of a complex system of values and practices: justice, prosperity, responsibility, toleration, cooperation, and peace. Many people believe that liberty is the core political value of modern civilization itself, the one that gives substance and form to all the other values of social life. They're called libertarians.

Libertarianism.org is the Cato Institute's treasury of resources about the theory and history of liberty. The book you're holding is a small part of what Libertarianism.org has to offer. In addition to hosting classic texts by historical libertarian figures and original articles from modern-day thinkers, Libertarianism.org publishes podcasts, videos, online introductory courses, and books on a variety of topics within the libertarian tradition.

Cato Institute

Founded in 1977, the Cato Institute is a public policy research foundation dedicated to broadening the parameters of policy debate to allow consideration of more options that are consistent with the principles of limited government, individual liberty, and peace. To that end, the Institute strives to achieve greater involvement of the intelligent, concerned lay public in questions of policy and the proper role of government.

The Institute is named for Cato's Letters, libertarian pamphlets that were widely read in the American Colonies in the early 18th century and played a major role in laying the philosophical foundation for the American Revolution.

Despite the achievement of the nation's Founders, today virtually no aspect of life is free from government encroachment. A pervasive intolerance for individual rights is shown by government's arbitrary intrusions into private economic transactions and its disregard for civil liberties. And while freedom around the globe has notably increased in the past several decades, many countries have moved in the opposite direction, and most governments still do not respect or safeguard the wide range of civil and economic liberties.

To address those issues, the Cato Institute undertakes an extensive publications program on the complete spectrum of policy issues. Books, monographs, and shorter studies are commissioned to examine the federal budget, Social Security, regulation, military spending, international trade, and myriad other issues. Major policy conferences are held throughout the year, from which papers are published thrice yearly in the *Cato Journal*. The Institute also publishes the quarterly magazine *Regulation*.

In order to maintain its independence, the Cato Institute accepts no government funding. Contributions are received from foundations, corporations, and individuals, and other revenue is generated from the sale of publications. The Institute is a nonprofit, tax-exempt, educational foundation under Section 501(c)3 of the Internal Revenue Code.

CATO INSTITUTE

1000 Massachusetts Ave., N.W.

Washington, D.C. 20001

www.cato.org